Microwave Magic
Seafood

Grolier Limited
TORONTO

Contributors to this series:

Recipes and Technical Assistance:
École de cuisine Bachand-Bissonnette
Cooking consultants:
Denis Bissonette
Michèle Émond
Dietician:
Christiane Barbeau
Photos:
Laramée Morel Communications
Audio-Visuelles
Design:
Claudette Taillefer
Assistants:
Julie Deslauriers
Philippe O'Connor
Joan Pothier
Accessories:
Andrée Cournoyer
Writing:
Communications La Griffe Inc.
Text Consultants:
Cap et bc inc.
Advisors:
Roger Aubin
Joseph R. De Varennes
Gaston Lavoie
Kenneth H. Pearson

Assembly:
Carole Garon
Vital Lapalme
Jean-Pierre Larose
Carl Simmons
Gus Soriano
Marc Vallières
Production Managers:
Gilles Chamberland
Ernest Homewood
Production Assistants:
Martine Gingras
Catherine Gordon
Kathy Kishimoto
Peter Thomlison
Art Director:
Bernard Lamy
Editors:
Laurielle Ilacqua
Susan Marshall
Margaret Oliver
Robin Rivers
Lois Rock
Jocelyn Smyth
Donna Thomson
Dolores Williams
Development:
Le Groupe Polygone Éditeurs Inc.

We wish to thank the following firms, PIER I IMPORTS and LE CACHE POT, for their contribution to the illustration of this set.

The series editors have taken every care to ensure that the information given is accurate. However, no cookbook can guarantee the user successful results. The editors cannot accept any responsibility for the results obtained by following the recipes and recommendations given.

Canadian Cataloguing in Publication Data

Main entry under title:

Seafood

(Microwave magic ; 6)
Translation of: Les Fruits de mer.
Includes index.
ISBN 0-7172-2427-9

1. Cookery (Seafood).   2. Microwave cookery.
I. Series: Microwave magic (Toronto, Ont.) ; 6.

TX832.F7713 1988   641.6'9   C88-094225-8

Contents

Microwave Magic is a multi-volume set, with each volume devoted to a particular type of cooking. So, if you are looking for a chicken recipe, you simply go to one of the two volumes that deal with poultry. Each volume has its own index, and the final volume contains a general index to the complete set.

Microwave Magic puts over twelve hundred recipes at your fingertips. You will find it as useful as the microwave oven itself. Enjoy!

Note from the Editor

How to Use this Book
The books in this set have been designed to make your job as easy as possible. As a result, most of the recipes are set out in a standard way.

We suggest that you begin by consulting the information chart for the recipe you have chosen. You will find there all the information you need to decide if you are able to make it: preparation time, cost per serving, level of difficulty, number of calories per serving and other relevant details. Thus, if you have only 30 minutes in which to prepare the evening meal, you will quickly be able to tell which recipe is possible and suits your schedule.

The list of ingredients is always clearly separated from the main text. When space allows, the ingredients are shown together in a photograph so that you can make sure you have them all without rereading the list—another way of saving your valuable time. In addition, for the more complex recipes we have supplied photographs of the key stages involved either in preparation or serving.

All the dishes in this book have been cooked in a 700 watt microwave oven. If your oven has a different wattage, consult the conversion chart that appears on the following page for cooking times in different types of oven. We would like to emphasize that the cooking times given in the book are a minimum. If a dish does not seem to be cooked enough, you may return it to the oven for a few more minutes. Also, the cooking time can vary according to your ingredients: their water and fat content, thickness, shape and even where they come from. We have therefore left a blank space on each recipe page in which you can note

the cooking time that suits you best. This will enable you to add a personal touch to the recipes that we suggest and to reproduce your best results every time.

Although we have put all the technical information together at the front of this book, we have inserted a number of boxed entries called **MICROTIPS** throughout to explain particular techniques. They are brief and simple, and will help you obtain successful results in your cooking.

With the very first recipe you try, you will discover just how simple microwave cooking can be and how often it depends on techniques you already use for cooking with a conventional oven. If cooking is a pleasure for you, as it is for us, it will be all the more so with a microwave oven. Now let's get on with the food.

The Editor

Key to the Symbols
For ease of reference, the following symbols have been used on the recipe information charts.

The pencil symbol ✏️🍎 is a reminder to write your cooking time in the space provided.

Level of Difficulty

🍴 Easy

🍴🍴 Moderate

🍴🍴🍴 Complex

Cost per Serving

$ Inexpensive

$ $ Moderate

$ $ $ Expensive

Power Levels

All the recipes in this book have been tested in a 700 watt oven. As there are many microwave ovens on the market with different power levels, and as the names of these levels vary from one manufacturer to another, we have decided to give power levels as a percentage. To adapt the power levels given here, consult the chart opposite and the instruction manual for your oven.

Generally speaking, if you have a 500 watt or 600 watt oven you should increase cooking times by about 30% over those given, depending on the actual length of time required. The shorter the original cooking time, the greater the percentage by which it must be lengthened. The 30% figure is only an average. Consult the chart for detailed information on this topic.

Power Levels

HIGH: 100% - 90%	Vegetables (except boiled potatoes and carrots) Soup Sauce Fruits Browning ground beef Browning dish Popcorn
MEDIUM HIGH: 80% - 70%	Rapid defrosting of precooked dishes Muffins Some cakes Hot dogs
MEDIUM: 60% - 50%	Cooking tender meat Cakes Fish Seafood Eggs Reheating Boiled potatoes and carrots
MEDIUM LOW: 40%	Cooking less tender meat Simmering Melting chocolate
DEFROST: 30% **LOW: 30% - 20%**	Defrosting Simmering Cooking less tender meat
WARM: 10%	Keeping food warm Allowing yeast dough to rise

Cooking Time Conversion Chart

700 watts	600 watts*
5 s	11 s
15 s	20 s
30 s	40 s
45 s	1 min
1 min	1 min 20 s
2 min	2 min 40 s
3 min	4 min
4 min	5 min 20 s
5 min	6 min 40 s
6 min	8 min
7 min	9 min 20 s
8 min	10 min 40 s
9 min	12 min
10 min	13 min 30 s
20 min	26 min 40 s
30 min	40 min
40 min	53 min 40 s
50 min	66 min 40 s
1 h	1 h 20 min

* There is very little difference in cooking times between 500 watt ovens and 600 watt ovens.

The Bountiful Sea

From the beginning of time the fertile sea has provided man with a plentiful source of nutrition. The seas contain twenty thousand types of fish and almost half a million different species of crustaceans and mollusks. Of course, not all of these species are edible, or even accessible—however, the wide range of crustaceans and mollusks that are available has inspired centuries of culinary art.

Crustaceans, notably lobster, shrimp and crab, and mollusks, such as oysters, scallops and mussels, are commonly referred to as shellfish, or seafood. Like fish, they are known to be very nutritious. They have extremely high mineral, protein and vitamin contents and contain few calories. They should therefore be part of every well-balanced diet.

Most seafood can be bought fresh or alive, the latter being the best assurance of quality. Each type of seafood is caught in a specific way; crayfish and lobster are caught in traps and shrimp, by trawling or with large nets, while prawns can be caught with a long net by hand when they are in season.

Seafood, like fish, appears to have been somewhat neglected in North American food culture, both in terms of consumption and in terms of the availability of recipes and cooking techniques. To give seafood its proper place, *Microwave Magic* offers this volume, dedicated exclusively to the preparation of crustaceans and mollusks. You will find that this book of recipes and techniques will quickly become indispensable.

You will learn how to prepare most of the delicious crustaceans and mollusks that are available. Our first offering, on page 24, is Lobster Thermidor, a recipe that brings out the fine, delicate flavor of the "king of crustaceans."

The fact that seafood can indeed be successfully prepared in the microwave oven and that the preparation is so fast and easy may surprise some. But just try a few of the succulent crab, clam, scallop, oyster, frog leg, snail and squid recipes that we suggest and you will be convinced. Everyday meals will become feasts. Some dishes, such as Paella (page 96) or the Captain's Plate, part of the "Entertaining" menu (page 98), are culinary triumphs to delight the finest palate.

Bon appétit!

Crustaceans

Crustaceans are much prized by gourmets because of their firm, sweet flesh, and seafood lovers particularly enjoy preparing special dishes with them. The common edible crustaceans include the lobster, crab, crayfish, spiny lobster and shrimp. These aquatic animals (some, freshwater and others, salt water) are egglaying and are characterized by their hard outer shell or "crust", which turns red on cooking. Their bodies are segmented and most are equipped with antennae.

The lobster, considered to be the most delicate of the crustaceans, is also the largest. Much of our lobster comes from the Atlantic provinces, where large quantities are caught. It is available canned or frozen but is best used fresh. The front claws, armed with two pincers (one being large and oval in shape and the other, more elongated) contain some of the most flavorful meat.

There are many different species of crab. The most widely available and the one most used in cooking is the snow crab, also called the spider crab. Like the lobster, its meat is very delicate and much appreciated by gourmets; it is found inside the shell surrounding the legs and claws and extracting it is a long and fastidious operation. Crabmeat is also available canned and frozen.

Less accessible is the crayfish, a small, freshwater crustacean with less edible meat than the lobster. It is nonetheless much appreciated by seafood lovers for its subtle and delicate flavor.

The spiny lobster, or langouste, differs from the lobster in the absence of claws and in the size of its tail, which is longer and larger in proportion to its body. Since most of the edible meat is concentrated in the tail, it is often the case that only that part of the spiny lobster is sold.

Prawns differ in appearance from shrimp, having more slender abdomens and longer legs but, in commercial trade, the names are sometimes used synonymously. The term "prawn" is usually applied to larger marine shrimp. The Dublin Bay prawn is a close relative of the lobster; its meat is also very delicate and flavorful and is concentrated mainly in the tail. Fresh or frozen, this meat can be prepared in many ways.

The shrimp is the smallest of our table crustaceans. There are many different varieties of shrimp, two of the most common being the gray shrimp and the sword shrimp.

Dubbed the "king of crustaceans," the lobster is without doubt the most prized of all shellfish. Alive, it is greenish-brown or bluish in color and its antennae have a tinge of red.

Crab can be purchased fresh or cooked, in the shell or shelled. It also comes frozen or canned. Its delicate meat makes it a highly prized food item.

Smaller than the lobster but larger than shrimp, some varieties of prawn can be close to 30 cm (1 ft) in length. The prawn's reddish color does not change when cooked. Its claws do not contain much meat but that in the tail is very flavorful.

The shrimp has a softer shell. When buying shrimp check that the tail is well turned in, the flesh firm, and that there is no disagreeable odor.

Buying Guide

Planning is essential to the success of any meal. When making your purchases, remember that the amount you need depends on more than the number of people who will be eating. You must take into account the appetites of your family members and guests, the way in which the crustaceans are to be prepared, and the amount of fat they contain. Consult the chart opposite before buying the shellfish needed to prepare a recipe.

Cleaning Crustaceans

It is strongly recommended that seafood be bought live so that its delicate flavor can be fully appreciated. Cleaning is thus an essential part of preparation. Only a few tools are needed for this operation to be successful —scissors, a brush, and a sharp knife, all of which are easy to obtain. Mollusks should be well scrubbed, rinsed under running water to eliminate any filaments or excess sand, and an oyster knife is needed to open some.

Recommended Quantities (per Serving)

North American lobster	675 g (1-1/2 lb)
Crab (unshelled) (shelled)	450 g (1 lb) 115 g (4 oz)
Crayfish	10
Spiny lobster	175 to 225 g (6 to 8 oz)
Prawn	115 g (4 oz)
Shrimp (unshelled) (shelled)	225 g (8 oz) 115 g (4 oz)

Time of Year Available in Canada

Lobster	September to the end of March, summer months
Crab	all year, depending on the region
Crayfish	mainly from November to April
Spiny lobster	mainly from November to April
Prawn	mainly from November to April
Shrimp	all year, depending on the region

MICROTIPS

Butterflying Shrimp

Shell the shrimp, leaving the last segment and tail in place. With a sharp knife or kitchen shears, split the bottom of the shrimp lengthwise, cutting deep enough to be able to remove the vein. Spread the shrimp open and, under running water, remove the vein. Dry with paper towel. If the butterflied shrimp is to stuffed, however, cut along the back, devein, and open.

Lobster

The best way to enjoy the incomparable taste of lobster is to buy it fresh and cook it yourself. When selecting a live lobster look for a greenish-brown or bluish color and reddish antennae. The fishmonger will, in most cases, have taped the claws for safety.

A lobster's vigor is a sign of its freshness; it should be very active and should curl its tail under when picked up.

When selecting from lobsters of equal size, choose the heaviest; lobsters that are light for their size have probably been underfed for several days and will therefore provide less meat. Fresh lobster should be

cooked as soon as possible, preferably the day it is purchased. In the meantime, keep it in the refrigerator crisper, loose, without water.

Shelling Cooked Lobster

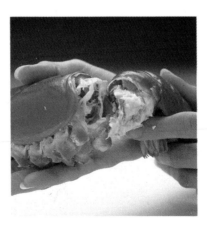

1. Let the cooked lobster cool. Remove the claws and legs with a sharp knife. Use a nut cracker to section the claws and the body and remove the meat.

2. Separate the tail from the body. With kitchen shears, cut away the membrane covering the underside. Remove the meat from the tail.

3. Hold the trunk in one hand. Split the underside with kitchen shears. Remove and discard the sac lodged between the eyes.

Crab

Of the many different varieties of crab found in North America, the most common is the spider or snow crab, weighing from 150 to 225 g (1/3 to 1/2 lb). Other highly valued varieties are the dormer crab, weighing between 800 g and 1.6 kg (1-3/4 to 3-1/2 lb), and the massive 2.7 to 9 kg (6 to 20 lb) Alaska king crab.

As with lobster, a live crab should be very active when you buy it. When picked up from behind, the crab should curl its claws in immediately. A slow reaction means that the crab is not in good health and should not be purchased. The abdomen of the female crab is covered with a membrane, called the apron, which is larger than that of the male; its purpose is to protect her eggs.

Crab is also sold cooked, in its shell or shelled. Crabmeat is available fresh, frozen, or canned as well. Soft-shell crabs, which are in season mainly during the summer, should be a blue-grey color and, cooked, will have a bright red shell. Cooked crabmeat, fresh or frozen, should be a clear white color, tinged with pink, and should be practically odorless.

Crab bought live should be cooked as quickly as possible. Before cooking,

however, it can be refrigerated in the same way as lobster. See page 16 for instructions on storing live crab.

Shelling Crab

Place the crab on a flat surface. Remove the claws and legs by twisting them off at the joint closest to the body shell. Carefully crack the shell of each claw and remove the meat.

Pull the membrane from the underside and remove the soft substance visible underneath. Insert the thumb between the shell and the body to separate them.

Remove the "dead man's fingers" (spongy white gills) and the digestive system from the middle of the body; they are not edible. With kitchen shears, break the body in half and remove the meat between the sections.

Shrimp

Shelling and Deveining Shrimp

Shrimp, one of the most common and well liked crustaceans, come in many varieties, each easily identified by size. The Nordic shrimp is 15 to 20 cm (6 to 8 in) long, the Nordic "American bouquet" shrimp, 7 to 12 cm (3 to 5 in) long, the sword shrimp, of exceptional quality, 6 to 12 cm (2-1/2 to 5 in) long, and the gray shrimp, the most flavorful of all, is 3 to 6 cm (1-1/4 to 2-1/2 in) long.

Shrimps are available all year round. They can be purchased fresh, canned or frozen. They come whole, breaded, cooked or raw. As with other crustaceans, it is important to check freshness when buying shrimp. The flesh should be firm and there should be no unpleasant odor.

The weight of fresh shrimp is reduced by half after shelling and cooking. For each serving, therefore, allow 225 g (1/2 lb) in the shell, 150 g (1/3 lb) shelled, or 115 g (1/4 lb) cooked and shelled.

Hold the shrimp in the left hand and pull the head off with the right hand.

With kitchen shears cut through the shell, 1.5 mm (1/16 in) deep, along the back.

Using your fingers, peel back the shell until the meat comes loose.

Hold the tail in one hand and carefully remove the meat from the shell, keeping the meat intact.

Gently pull to free the meat.

Hold the shelled shrimp under running water and remove the intestinal tract, commonly referred to as the "vein", with the fingertips.

15

Storing Crustaceans

Since fresh crustaceans are very perishable, it is best to prepare them as quickly as possible after purchase. Some crustaceans can be stored for brief periods but certain precise guidelines must be followed (see chart opposite).

Storing Crustaceans

Type	Duration	Method of Storing
Lobster or crayfish, live	2 days	In the refrigerator, loose in the crisper, without water
Crab, live	2 days	In the refrigerator, loose in the crisper, without water
Spiny lobster	2 days	In the refrigerator, loose in the crisper, without water
Shrimp	3 days	In the refrigerator, sealed tight in a bag

Defrosting Crustaceans

A unique feature of the microwave oven is that it enables you to defrost crustaceans quickly, without starting the cooking process. Simply follow the basic instructions given in the chart opposite.

You should always defrost at 30% power, turning and separating the pieces of shellfish and removing them from the microwave oven as they defrost. It is important to let the shellfish stand for 10 minutes to continue defrosting. Then rinse with cold water before beginning the recipe.

Defrosting Crustaceans

Type	Quantity	Power	Time (min)	Standing Time (min)	Comments
Lobster	225 g (8 oz)	30%	5-7	10	Remove from package and place in dish.
Crab legs	225 g (8 oz)	30%	5-7	10	Arrange on glass plate. Separate and turn over once.
Crabmeat	175 g (6 oz)	30%	4-5	10	Defrost in dish, without unpacking. Separate and turn over once.
Crayfish	175 g (6 oz)	30%	4-5	10	Defrost in dish, without unpacking. Separate and turn over once.
Prawns	175 g (6 oz)	30%	4-5	10	Remove from package and place in dish.
Shrimp	450 g (1 lb)	30%	3-4	10	Unpack and place in dish. Spread evenly and remove when defrosted.

Cooking Crustaceans

Microwave cooking is ideal for preparing crustaceans. In fact, most crustaceans come equipped with their own microwave-safe container, their shells, which become red when cooked. With this protection, the delicate meat retains its texture and fine flavor.

Generally, shellfish are cooked when the meat is opaque in color and firm in texture. Since the microwaves work very quickly on this type of meat, it is essential to check the cooking process at regular intervals during the suggested cooking time. When cooking is completed, be sure to let the shellfish stand for 5 minutes.

Cooking Times for Crustaceans

Type	Quantity	Power	Cooking Time
Lobster tails	1 at 225 g (8 oz)	100%	5-6 min
	2 at 225 g (8 oz)	100%	8-9 min
	4 at 225 g (8 oz)	100%	11-13 min
Crab legs	225-280 g (8-10 oz)	100%	5-6 min
	450-565 g (16-20 oz)	100%	8-9 min
Shrimp	200 g (7 oz)	70%	3-4 min
	450 g (1 lb)	70%	5-7 min

Mollusks

Mollusks are found in abundance in every region of the globe; they live in the sea, in fresh water and in humid ground. They are soft-bodied, unsegmented animals, most having a hard outer shell. Their size varies considerably from type to type, extending from 1 to 2 mm (the tiny periwinkle) to several meters (e.g., the octopus) in length. Those mollusks having shells can be divided into two main categories: bivalve mollusks, such as oysters, mussels, clams and scallops, and univalve mollusks, such as snails, periwinkles, sea mollusks, and terrestrial mollusks. Another mollusk family, known as cephalopods, includes the squid, cuttlefish and the octopus. Although long ignored in the kitchen, mollusks are extremely nutritious and are considered by some as belonging to a "choice" food category.

Oysters hold first place among mollusks. Oyster lovers eat them raw, served on a bed of ice with lemon, or they eat them smoked. Oysters can be used in soups, in casseroles, au gratin, as a garnish for fish or as delicious additions to stuffings.

Mussels, like other mollusks, are found in seas all over the world but are best from cold regions. Popular belief has it that mussels should not be eaten from the beginning of May to the end of August, that is, in those months without the letter "r". This belief is unfounded as, in fact, mussels are available throughout the year; just make sure you buy them very fresh. If you gather mussels yourself, be sure that the water does not contain any toxic material. Cockles, which resemble mussels, are less common in North America.

Clams are not as widely consumed as oysters, but their taste is nonetheless much appreciated by many. They may be eaten cooked or raw. They are frequently used to garnish cooked dishes and are added to soups and fish stews.

Scallops are known for both their delicate meat and their distinctive shell. The scallop is frequently removed from its shell and immediately frozen and is therefore sometimes difficult to obtain fresh. Scallops may be prepared in many different ways.

Snails have become better known in the last few years. They are mainly available cooked and tinned in their own liquid. Known as "escargots" on restaurant menus, they are often served in the shell with garlic butter, which enhances their flavor.

The periwinkle is a small sea snail with a smooth shell. Its meat is delicate and much prized; in some regions it is served as an hors d'oeuvre, either plain or marinated. It can also be served boiled in the shell with spices and condiments.

Buying Guide

Buying Guide

It may seem difficult to judge the quantity required for one serving of seafood, especially when serving mollusks. The chart opposite is a useful guide to serving quantities. Of course, these quantities may be adjusted according to the appetites and tastes of your family and guests.

Storing Mollusks

Except for oysters, which can be kept up to two weeks in the refrigerator (if freshly harvested), and snails, generally bought cooked and canned, mollusks should be consumed as quickly as possible after purchase.

Recommended Quantities (per Serving)

Type	Quantity
Oysters	
— as hors d'oeuvres	6 to 12
— as main course, stuffed	4 to 6
Mussels	
— small	18 to 24
— large	12
Clams	16 to 20
Scallops	150 g (5 oz)
Snails	
— small	12 to 24
— large	6 to 12
Frogs' legs	6 to 12, depending on size

Mussels can be kept for 24 hours in the refrigerator before cooking but should be wrapped in a damp cloth. The fact that some mussels will open while being stored in this way does not mean that they are no longer fresh. When removing them from the refrigerator give them a gentle tap; most will close up but discard any mussel that remains open.

Scallops should also be prepared within 24 hours, unless they are frozen, in which case they may be stored for up to 3 months. Note, however, that most "fresh" scallops have been frozen and should not be refrozen.

Clams, if bought fresh, should be prepared as soon as possible after purchase. If wrapped carefully and refrigerated they will stay fresh for up to 24 hours.

MICROTIPS

Freezing and Defrosting Mollusks

If well wrapped, and preferably vacuum-packed, most mollusks can be kept in the freezer for up to 3 months without drying out or losing their freshness. Remove them from the shell before freezing. Mussels, however, must be cooked before freezing.

Mollusks defrost well in the microwave oven. To defrost 340 g (12 oz) of oysters, simply unwrap them and heat at 30% for 3 to 4 minutes, moving them several times during the defrosting time, and removing them from the oven as they defrost. Let stand for 5 minutes.

To defrost 450 g (1 lb) of scallops, leave them in their wrapping if they are frozen in a block but spread them out if they are loose. Heat at 30% for 8 to 10 minutes, moving them several times during defrosting and removing them as they defrost. Let stand for 5 minutes.

Buying Scallops

If bought frozen, scallops generally need only to be rinsed under running water before cooking. If fresh from the fishmonger they are usually already shelled, but it may be necessary for you to remove the small black vein around the meat. Simply cut it off with a sharp knife and rinse the meat before beginning the recipe.

Oysters

1. Wrap the oyster in a folded cloth and set it on a flat surface. Holding the oyster firmly, insert the blade of an oyster knife into the small opening at the center of the hinge. Twist the blade and separate the shells.

2. Still holding the oyster, slip the blade of the oyster knife more deeply into the gap between the shells and slit the ligament. Retaining as much liquor as possible, remove the top shell. Discard any broken shell.

3. Hold the bottom shell and slide the blade along the shell, under the oyster, to slit the muscle holding it to the shell. Remove the oyster.

Safety First

You must exercise special caution when gathering mussels yourself, as they may be toxic if gathered in polluted water. The mussel feeds itself by filtering the minerals and so on from the water surrounding it; it would therefore be contaminated by polluted water and would be toxic for humans. For this reason, it is important to gather mussels only in approved areas.

MICROTIPS

Add Variety to Shrimp Dishes

Try serving shrimps with different garnishes or sauces. Shrimps Danish Style is a delicious mixture of asparagus and shrimp. Combine asparagus tips with large cooked shrimp, place in a ramekin, and coat with store-bought shrimp sauce. Heat at 100% for 4 minutes and serve.

Clams

1. Clams are fresh when they resist opening. First, scrub them under running water to remove any sand.

2. Insert the point of an oyster knife into the small opening at the hinge. Push the knife in more deeply and pry the shells apart with a twisting motion. Discard the upper shell.

3. Cut the meat loose from the bottom shell and remove any particles of broken shell.

MICROTIPS

Defrosting Shrimp

Small crustaceans are more vulnerable to freezer burn than larger ones and, for this reason, they must be very carefully wrapped before freezing.

Because they are so small, shrimps can be defrosted by spreading them in a single layer in the bottom of a dish. The microwaves are thus evenly distributed and defrosting is very fast. See the chart on page 16 for defrosting information. Like all other crustaceans, shrimps should be kept frozen until they are to be used.

Removing Filaments from Mussels

Mussels fresh from the fishmonger's may not have been perfectly cleaned and some filaments may remain attached to the shells.

This filament, called the byssus or beard, attaches the mussel to the rocks. Make sure the filament is removed during the cleaning operation, which consists of scrubbing the mussel under cold running water to remove any sand. The byssus can be removed by pulling or, if it resists, by cutting it with a knife.

Cooking Mollusks

Mollusks need very little cooking to retain their delicate flavor; overcooking will ruin the best recipe. The liquid in bivalve mollusks, such as oysters, mussels, clams, and scallops, is released quickly during microwave cooking; for this reason, it is possible to cook them in a casserole in their own natural liquor, with no added ingredients. Of course, many delicious recipes with a number of complementary ingredients have been developed to enhance the flavor and perfume the scent of these shellfish.

Scrub the mussels, remove the byssus and rinse them. Place the mussels in a casserole and add any suggested ingredients.

Place the dish in the oven and cook as indicated in the recipe. The mussel shells will open when heated by the microwaves.

When cooking is completed remove and discard any unopened mussels.

MICROTIPS

Serving Mollusks

The way to present mussels at the table depends on whether they are served with or without their shells. Mussels in their shells are generally served in a shallow bowl with their natural cooking juices. Oysters, on the other hand, look their best when the shells are arranged symmetrically on a round plate, with their narrow ends pointing toward the center.

Less Familiar Seafood

Although the sea urchin, cuttlefish, squid, octopus, frog and eel are less familiar forms of seafood, they nonetheless possess qualities that are greatly appreciated by certain people.

The sea urchin may be eaten raw or cooked and it is frequently used in the preparation of coulis and sauces. It has a special taste, making it the ideal garnish for certain types of fish and seafood.

Cuttlefish, squid and octopus are all cephalopods and are equipped with a group of muscular arms and a sac containing an ink, called sepia, which they can release when threatened. Some recipes call for the sepia as an ingredient in the preparation of these marine animals. The preparation of this type of seafood is no more time consuming than that of most shellfish, but only the tentacles and the body sac are edible. If you are not familiar with this form of seafood, try the recipe for Squid Stuffed with Ham on page 86 of this volume.

Most people are more familiar with the frog, although only the legs are eaten. Its meat is light, tasty and easy to digest. Frogs' legs are available from the fishmonger, fresh or frozen, and are often prepared "à la provençale" (see the recipe on page 72).

MICROTIPS

Killing Lobster

Some recipes require that the lobster be cut into pieces while it is still alive. This procedure is not difficult, if certain specific techniques are followed. First, place the lobster on a flat surface. With a very sharp chef's knife sever the spinal cord by slicing the back of the head

with a firm blow. Then cut the lobster, lengthwise, in two, and remove the inedible sac and intestine. You may wish to reserve the coral, the green creamy substance found in the trunk, and mix it with melted butter. Detach the tail and cut into two sections and crack the claws to remove the meat.

Lobster Thermidor

Level of Difficulty	🍴🍴🍴
Preparation Time	30 min
Cost per Serving	$ $ $
Number of Servings	2
Nutritional Value	501 calories 29.5 g protein 37.9 g lipids
Food Exchanges	5 oz meat 1/2 bread exchange 2 fat exchanges
Cooking Time	3 min 40 sec
Standing Time	None
Power Level	100%
Write Your Cooking Time Here	

Ingredients

1 lobster, 900 g (2 lb), cooked
30 mL (2 tablespoons) butter
30 mL (2 tablespoons) green onions, finely chopped
15 mL (1 tablespoon) flour
15 mL (1 tablespoon) dry sherry
15 mL (1 tablespoon) white wine
50 mL (1/4 cup) fish stock
60 mL (4 tablespoons) Parmesan cheese, grated
15 mL (1 tablespoon) parsley, chopped
15 mL (1 tablespoon) 35% cream
5 mL (1 teaspoon) Dijon mustard
salt and pepper to taste

⇒

Lobster Thermidor

Assemble the ingredients required for this recipe, one that lobster lovers will thoroughly enjoy.

To cook the lobster, place it in a microwave-safe dish and cover with plastic wrap.

Once cooked, break off the claws and set aside.

With a long, sharp knife split the lobster shell in two, lengthwise.

Gently pull the cooked meat from the split shell.

Clean the shell and set aside to fill before serving.

Method
— Remove the lobster meat and cut into 1.5 cm (1/2 in) cubes; set the shell aside.
— Melt the butter in a casserole at 100% for 40 seconds, add the green onion, and cook at 100% for 1 minute.
— Stir in the flour and add the sherry, white wine and fish stock; mix well to obtain a smooth consistency and cook at 100% for 2 minutes, stirring after 1 minute.
— Add half the Parmesan cheese and the parsley, cream and Dijon mustard. Season with salt and pepper.
— Mix well, until the cheese has melted.
— Replace the lobster meat in the shell, coat with the sauce, and sprinkle with the remaining Parmesan cheese before serving.
— Reheat, if necessary, at 100% for 1 minute or until heated through.

Sauces

A Sauce for Every Taste and Every Occasion

The flavor of any dish, from the simplest of recipes to those requiring the most complex preparation, is largely defined by its sauce. Sauces play an important role in joining the subtle scent and flavor of any food. They enhance the taste of the dish being prepared or add a certain *je-ne-sais-quoi*, transforming it into one that your guests will remember.

In this book we present recipes with sauces to satisfy a wide range of tastes, trends and occasions. Some recipes are traditional and well-known favorites; others enable you to familiarize yourself with new sauces or to try new combinations of ingredients—ones that may well never have occurred to you. All of these recipes are conducive to your discovering the special characteristics of crustaceans and mollusks when cooked in the microwave oven. And now, it's up to you to explore these new avenues in the unlimited world of culinary art!

Lobster Meat au Gratin

Level of Difficulty	🍴🍴
Preparation Time	20 min
Cost per Serving	$ $ $
Number of Servings	4
Nutritional Value	308 calories 22.6 g protein 22.6 g lipids
Food Exchanges	3 oz meat 2 fat exchanges
Cooking Time	8 min
Standing Time	3 min
Power Level	70%
Write Your Cooking Time Here	

Ingredients
4 lobsters, 450 g (1 lb) each, cooked
175 mL (3/4 cup) 35% cream
30 mL (2 tablespoons) tomato paste
salt and pepper to taste
2 mL (1/2 teaspoon) thyme
75 mL (1/3 cup) Gruyère cheese, grated
30 mL (2 tablespoons) parsley, chopped

Method
— Remove the meat from each lobster shell and cut into cubes of equal size.
— Place the cooked meat in a baking dish and set aside.
— In another dish, combine the cream and the tomato paste, add the salt and pepper, and then add the thyme.
— Pour this sauce over the lobster meat, sprinkle with the Gruyère cheese and the parsley.
— Cook uncovered at 70% for 6 to 8 minutes, or until hot, giving the dish a half-turn halfway through the cooking time.
— Let stand for 3 minutes before serving.

Assemble all the ingredients for this tasty, easy-to-make recipe.

Remove the meat from the lobster shell and spread evenly in the bottom of a baking dish.

Pour the sauce over the lobster and cook, uncovered, at 70% for 6 to 8 minutes. Give the dish a half-turn halfway through the cooking time.

29

Stuffed Lobster Tails

Level of Difficulty	🍴🍴
Preparation Time	15 min
Cost per Serving	$ $ $
Number of Servings	2
Nutritional Value	297 calories 20.5 g protein 19.2 g lipids
Food Exchanges	3 oz meat 2 fat exchanges 1/2 bread exchange
Cooking Time	13 min
Standing Time	5 min
Power Level	70%, 100%
Write Your Cooking Time Here	

Ingredients
2 lobster tails, 225 g (1/2 lb) each
45 mL (3 tablespoons) butter, melted
50 mL (1/4 cup) breadcrumbs
onion powder to taste
paprika to taste
salt to taste

Lemon Butter:
125 mL (1/2 cup) butter
45 mL (3 tablespoons) lemon juice

Method
— With strong, sharp kitchen shears, cut the entire length of the shell on the underside of the lobster tails.
— Lift the meat from the shell, leaving it attached to the tail at its extremity.
— Put into a microwave-safe dish, placing the fleshy part of each tail so that it faces the outside of the dish.
— Mix the melted butter with the breadcrumbs, onion powder, paprika and salt. Spread the mixture over the lobster tails.
— Cover and cook at 70% for 4 minutes. Without uncovering, give the dish a half-turn and continue to cook at 70% for another 4 to 6 minutes, or until the meat is cooked.
— Let stand for 5 minutes. In the meantime, prepare the lemon butter by mixing the butter and lemon juice and cooking it at 100% for 2 to 3 minutes. Pour the melted butter over the lobster tails and serve.

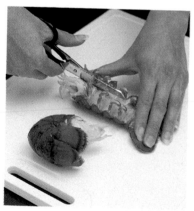

Cut along the shell on the underside of each lobster tail from the base to the extremity.

Lift the meat from the shell, leaving it attached at the end of the tail.

Spread the other ingredients over the lobster tails and cook as directed in the recipe.

Shrimps Creole

Level of Difficulty	🍴🍴🍴
Preparation Time	15 min
Cost per Serving	$ $
Number of Servings	4
Nutritional Value	195 calories 25.3 g protein 1.1 g lipids
Food Exchanges	3 oz meat 1 vegetable exchange
Cooking Time	18 min
Standing Time	5 min
Power Level	100%, 70%
Write Your Cooking Time Here	

Ingredients
450 g (1 lb) shrimps, fresh or defrosted
1 onion, finely chopped
1 medium green pepper, finely chopped
125 mL (1/2 cup) celery, finely chopped
1 clove garlic, minced
1 796 mL (28 oz) can tomatoes, drained and chopped
1 156 (5-1/2 oz) can tomato paste
10 mL (2 teaspoons) dried parsley
1 mL (1/4 teaspoon) thyme
1 bay leaf
pinch cayenne pepper

Method
— Combine the onion, green pepper, celery and garlic.
— Place in a microwave-safe dish, cover, and cook at 100% for 2 to 3 minutes, stirring halfway through the cooking time.
— Add all the other ingredients except the shrimp, and mix well.
— Cover and cook at 100% for 5 minutes.
— Stir and cook for another 5 minutes at 100%.
— Add the shrimps, cover and reduce the power to 70%; cook for 4 to 5 minutes, stirring halfway through the cooking time.
— Let stand for 5 minutes before serving.

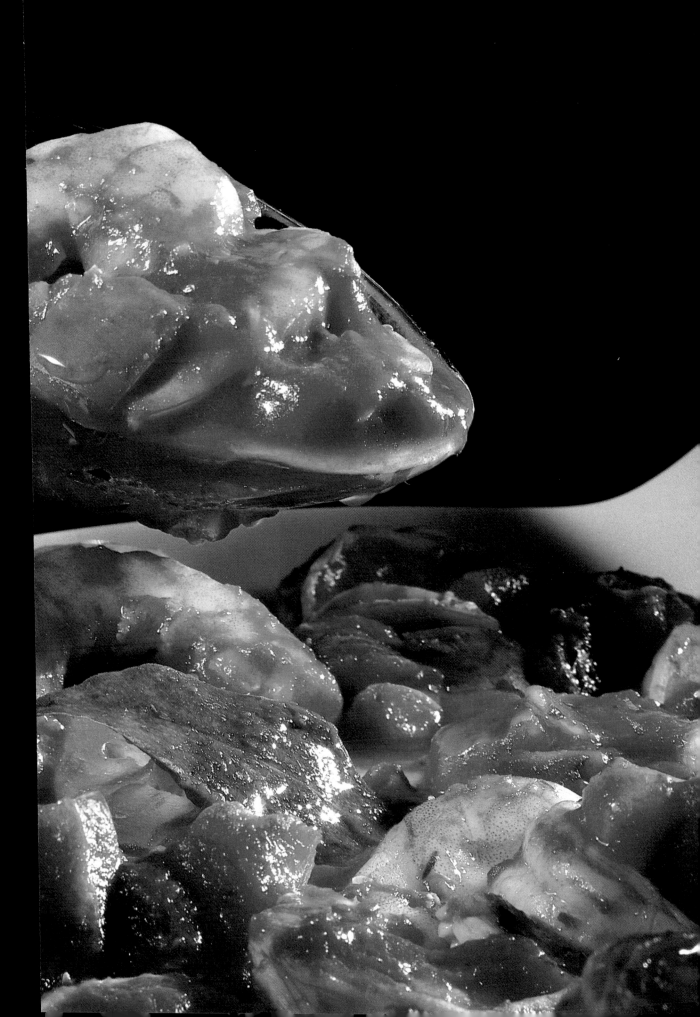

Shrimps with Garlic Butter

Level of Difficulty	🍴
Preparation Time	15 min
Cost per Serving	$ $ $
Number of Servings	4
Nutritional Value	416 calories 43 g protein 24.8 g lipids
Food Exchanges	5 oz meat 1 fat exchange 1 bread exchange
Cooking Time	11 min
Standing Time	3 min
Power Level	100%, 70%
Write Your Cooking Time Here	

Ingredients
900 g (2 lb) fresh shrimps
125 mL (1/2 cup) butter
5 cloves garlic, crushed
50 mL (1/4 cup) fresh parsley, finely chopped
30 mL (2 tablespoons) lemon juice

Method
— Shell, devein, and clean the shrimps; arrange in a round dish, placing the thicker parts so that they face the outer edge of the dish.
— In another dish, melt the butter at 100% for 1-1/2 to 2 minutes, add the crushed garlic, parsley and lemon juice.
— Cook at 100% for 2 to 3 minutes and pour over the uncooked shrimps.
— Reduce the power level to 70%, cover, and cook for 5 to 6 minutes, giving the dish a half-turn halfway through the cooking time.
— Let stand for 3 minutes before serving.
— Serve with 125 mL (1/2 cup) of rice per person.

Shell and devein the fresh shrimps and rinse well.

Pour the cooked garlic butter over the uncooked shrimps and proceed as directed in the recipe.

MICROTIPS

Shelling Fresh Shrimp

Hold the shrimp and twist to detach the head. Using your fingers, separate the shell on the underside (at the legs) and, holding the tail firmly, gently pull the shrimp free of the shell.

Shrimps Chinese Style

Level of Difficulty	🍴
Preparation Time	15 min
Cost per Serving	$ $ $
Number of Servings	4
Nutritional Value	150 calories 23.7 g protein 0.9 g lipids
Food Exchanges	2 oz meat 1 vegetable exchange
Cooking Time	6 min
Standing Time	5 min
Power Level	100%, 70%
Write Your Cooking Time Here	

Ingredients
450 g (1 lb) medium-sized shrimps
15 mL (1 tablespoon) oil
1 onion, cut into strips
1 red pepper, cut into strips
1 green pepper, cut into strips
1 small cucumber, cut into strips
250 mL (1 cup) mushrooms, sliced
15 mL (1 tablespoon) soy sauce
1 tomato, cut into eighths

Method
— Shell and devein the shrimps; set aside.
— Preheat a browning dish at 100% for 7 minutes.
— In the meantime, cut the vegetables into strips.
— Pour the oil into the browning dish and heat at 100% for 30 seconds.
— Sear the shrimps, remove from the dish, and set aside.
— Reheat the browning dish at 100% for 3 minutes.
— Sear all the vegetables except the tomatoes, and then add the shrimps.
— Cover, reduce the power to 70% and cook for 4 to 5 minutes, stirring halfway through the cooking time.
— Stir in the soy sauce and the tomato pieces.
— Let stand for 5 minutes before serving.

Assemble all the ingreients needed for this oriental style dish.

Sear the shrimp by tossing quickly in the preheated browning dish; remove from the dish and set aside.

When the shrimp and vegetable mixture is cooked, add the soy sauce and the tomatoes.

Shrimps American Style

Level of Difficulty	🍴
Preparation Time	10 min
Cost per Serving	$ $
Number of Servings	4
Nutritional Value	265 calories 32.9 g protein 8.4 g lipids
Food Exchanges	3 oz meat 1 fat exchange
Cooking Time	7 min
Standing Time	3 min
Power Level	70%
Write Your Cooking Time Here	

Ingredients
675 g (1-1/2 lb) shrimps, shelled and deveined
15 mL (1 tablespoon) onion, chopped

15 mL (1 tablespoon) celery, chopped
125 mL (1/2 cup) tomatoes, crushed
30 mL (2 tablespoons)

tomato paste
125 mL (1/2 cup) prepared brown sauce
5 mL (1 teaspoon) tarragon
garlic, salt, pepper and cayenne to taste
60 to 90 mL (2 to 3 oz) cognac

Method
— Arrange the shrimps on a plate, placing the thicker parts so that they face the outer edge.
— In another dish, combine all the other ingredients and pour the mixture over the shrimps.
— Cover and cook at 70% for 5 to 7 minutes, giving the plate a half-turn halfway through the cooking time.
— Let stand for 3 minutes before serving.

MICROTIPS

For Delicious Leftovers

Cooked seafood leftovers can be divided into individual servings and reheated in microwave-safe dishes one or two days later.

Cover the dishes with plastic wrap, store in the refrigerator, and reheat at 70% for 2 to 3 minutes, or until heated through.

You can also freeze seafood leftovers for up to one month. Try covering the leftovers

with the reserved cooking juices before freezing and, when defrosted and reheated, your seafood will be as tasty as when it was first prepared.

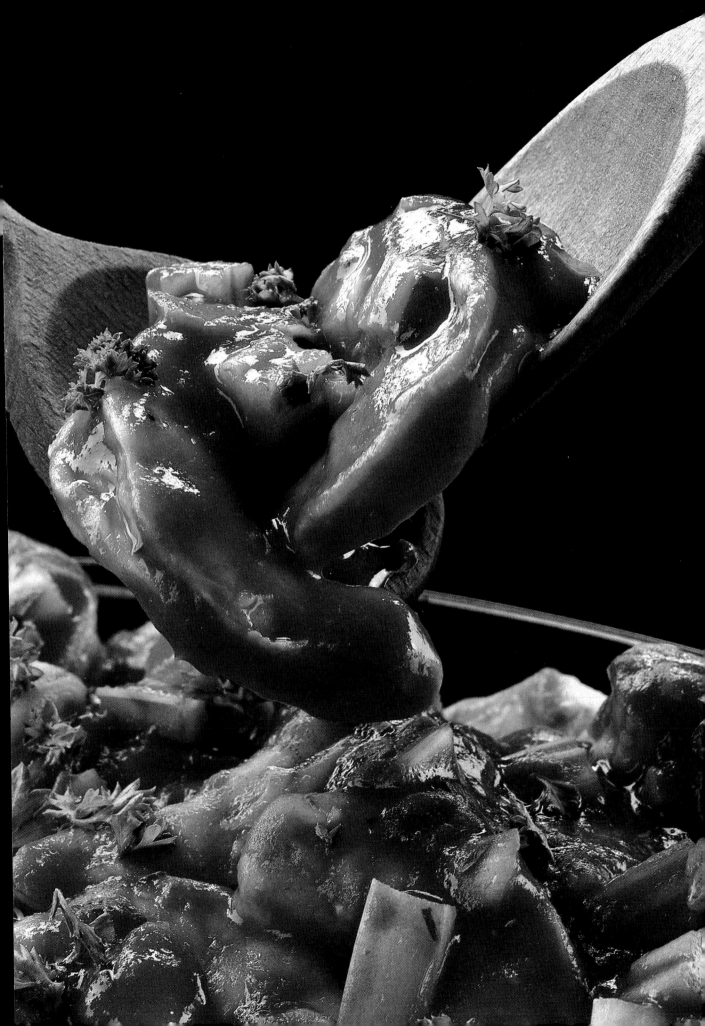

Shrimps with Coconut

Level of Difficulty	🍴🔪
Preparation Time	20 min
Cost per Serving	$ $
Number of Servings	8
Nutritional Value	183 calories 22.9 g protein 7.6 g lipids
Food Exchanges	3 oz meat 1/2 fat exchange
Cooking Time	17 min
Standing Time	None
Power Level	90%, 100%
Write Your Cooking Time Here	

Ingredients
900 g (2 lb) fresh shrimps, shelled and deveined
250 mL (1 cup) chicken stock
125 mL (1/2 cup) 18% cream
75 mL (1/3 cup) coconut, grated
75 mL (1/3 cup) onion, chopped
125 mL (1/2 cup) celery, chopped
1 clove garlic, crushed
30 mL (2 tablespoons) butter
15 mL (1 tablespoon) curry powder
30 mL (2 tablespoons) flour
5 mL (1 teaspoon) Worcestershire sauce
pinch of crushed chili peppers
5 mL (1 teaspoon) lemon zest, grated
30 mL (2 tablespoons) lemon juice
15 mL (1 tablespoon) parsley

Method
— Arrange the shrimps on a plate, placing the thicker parts so that they face the outer edge and any smaller shrimps in the center.
— Cover and cook at 90% for 4 minutes, giving the dish a half-turn halfway through the cooking time.
— Drain the liquid from the plate and set the shrimps aside.
— Combine the chicken stock, cream and coconut and heat at 100% for 2 minutes; stir well and set aside.
— Combine the onion, celery, garlic and butter and cook at 100% for 2 minutes; stir and continue to cook at 100% for 1 minute.
— Add the remaining ingredients to the cooked vegetables and mix well.
— Pour the chicken stock, cream and coconut mixture over the cooked vegetables; cook at 100% for 3 to 4 minutes, or until the mixture becomes thick, stirring after 2

minutes.
— Add the shrimps and cook at 90% for 3 to 4 minutes, stirring once during the cooking time.

Arrange the shrimps on a microwave-safe plate, placing the fleshy parts so that they face the outside of the plate.

Combine the vegetables cook as directed in the recipe, and pour the mixture of chicken stock, cream and coconut over them.

Prawns with Garlic Butter

Level of Difficulty	🍴🍴
Preparation Time	20 min
Cost per Serving	$ $ $
Number of Servings	4
Nutritional Value	287 calories 14.8 g protein 24.6 g lipids
Food Exchanges	2.5 oz meat 2 fat exchanges
Cooking Time	14 min
Standing Time	5 min
Power Level	100%, 70%
Write Your Cooking Time Here	

Ingredients
450 g (1 lb) fresh prawns
30 mL (2 tablespoons) lemon juice
125 mL (1/2 cup) butter
50 mL (1/4 cup) parsley, finely chopped
5 cloves garlic, crushed

Method
— Clean the prawns well; slit the top shell lengthwise and devein.
— Arrange the prawns on a plate, sprinkle with lemon juice, and set aside.
— Melt the butter at 100% for 1-1/2 to 2 minutes; add the parsley and garlic, mix well, and cook at 100% for 2 to 3 minutes.
— Pour the butter, parsley and garlic mixture over the prawns; cover and cook at 70% for 7 to 9 minutes, giving the plate a half-turn halfway through the cooking time.
— Let stand for 5 minutes before serving.

⟹

Prawns with Garlic Butter

With kitchen shears slit the top shell lengthwise.

Devein the prawn by removing the black filament that runs along the flesh.

Give the plate a half-turn halfway through the cooking time to ensure uniform cooking.

MICROTIPS

Aioli—A Delicious Sauce from Provence

Aioli is a garlic mayonnaise from the Provence region of France which goes beautifully with hot or cold poached fish. Indeed, poached cod served with aioli is a traditional speciality of Provence. Aioli is quick to prepare and requires no cooking. Be sure that the oil and the eggs are at room temperature before proceeding as directed below.

1. Crush the garlic cloves (2 per serving) and add a pinch of salt. Stirring constantly, slowly add the egg yolks (1 per serving). Continue stirring until the egg yolks become light in color.

2. Use 150 to 200 mL (2/3 cup or more) of oil per egg yolk. Add the oil, drop by drop, beating vigorously with a wire whisk until the sauce thickens. Then pour the oil in a steady stream, continuing to beat.

3. Stop beating when all the oil has been added. Add a few drops of lemon juice and 15 mL (1 tablespoon) of lukewarm water. Mix well, then add more oil if required to make the sauce thick enough to spoon without running.

Prawns Italian Style

Ingredients

450 g (1 lb) fresh prawns
50 mL (1/4 cup) olive oil
5 cloves garlic, crushed
125 mL (1/2 cup) tomatoes, peeled, seeded, and chopped
15 mL (1 tablespoon) parsley, chopped
5 mL (1 teaspoon) oregano
2 mL (1/2 teaspoon) pepper

Level of Difficulty	🍴🍴
Preparation Time	20 min
Cost per Serving	$ $ $
Number of Servings	2
Nutritional Value	425 calories 29.3 g protein 62.5 g lipids
Food Exchanges	4 oz meat 2 fat exchanges
Cooking Time	14 min
Standing Time	5 min
Power Level	100%, 70%
Write Your Cooking Time Here	

Method

— Heat the oil and garlic in a dish at 100% for 2 minutes.
— Add all the other ingredients except the prawns; cook at 100% for 2 to 3 minutes, mix well, and set aside.
— Prepare the prawns by splitting the shell in two lengthwise, leaving the last segment in place so as to be able to spread the shell open like butterfly wings.
— Arrange the prawns on a plate and coat them evenly with the tomato mixture.
— Cover and cook at 70% for 7 to 9 minutes, giving the plate a half-turn halfway through the cooking time.
— Let stand for 5 minutes before serving.

Prawns in Potato Boats

Level of Difficulty	
Preparation Time	15 min
Cost per Serving	$ $ $
Number of Servings	4
Nutritional Value	389 calories 36.7 g protein 14.7 g lipids
Food Exchanges	5 oz meat 1 fat exchange 1 bread exchange
Cooking Time	17 min
Standing Time	3 min
Power Level	100%, 70%
Write Your Cooking Time Here	

Ingredients
24 prawns, shelled, deveined, and cooked
4 large potatoes
45 mL (3 tablespoons) butter
45 mL (3 tablespoons) flour
250 mL (1 cup) fish stock
250 mL (1 cup) milk
pepper to taste
50 mL (1/4 cup) grated Parmesan cheese
parsley, chopped

Method
— Arrange the potatoes on a plate and cook at 100% for 6 to 7 minutes.
— Split the potatoes lengthwise and scoop out the pulp, leaving a 0.5 cm (1/4 in) layer to keep the shell stiff. (Set the excess pulp aside for later use, e.g., potato purée.)
— Melt the butter in a casserole at 100% for 40 seconds; add the flour and mix.
— Stir in the fish stock, milk and pepper; mix well and cook at 100% for 5 to 6 minutes, or until the sauce thickens, stirring every 2 minutes.
— Cut the prawns into pieces, add to the sauce, and stuff each potato shell with the mixture.
— Sprinkle with Parmesan cheese and parsley; cook uncovered at 70% for 3 to 4 minutes, giving the plate a half-turn halfway through the cooking time.
— Let stand for 3 minutes before serving.

After cooking the potatoes, split lengthwise and scoop out the inside.

Add the pieces of prawn to the cooked sauce.

Stuff the potatoes with the mixture and cook at 70% for 3 to 4 minutes, giving the plate a half-turn halfway through the cooking time.

Seafood Salad

Level of Difficulty	🍴
Preparation Time	20 min*
Cost per Serving	$ $
Number of Servings	6
Nutritional Value	219 calories 26.9 g protein 9.1 g lipids
Food Exchanges	3 oz meat 1 vegetable exchange 1 fat exchange
Cooking Time	7 min
Standing Time	None
Power Level	100%, 70%
Write Your Cooking Time Here	

* Allow the salad to chill completely before serving.

Ingredients
450 g (1 lb) fresh squid
450 g (1 lb) fresh shrimps
15 mL (1 tablespoon) butter
30 mL (2 tablespoons) onion, grated
1 clove garlic, curshed
15 mL (1 tablespoon) roasted red pepper, chopped
1 mL (1/4 teaspoon) rosemary
salt and pepper to taste
125 mL (1/2 cup) lemon juice
1 avocado, peeled and cut into cubes
250 mL (1 cup) celery, thinly sliced
6 large lettuce leaves
parsley, chopped

Method
— Clean the squid, cut into 1.5 cm (1/2 in) thick pieces, and set aside.
— Shell, devein and clean the shrimps, cut in half, and set aside.
— Melt the butter in a dish at 100% for 30 seconds; add the onion, garlic, red pepper, rosemary, salt and pepper. Cook at 100% for 1-1/2 minutes.

— Arrange the squid and shrimp pieces on a plate and cover with the seasoned onion mixture.
— Reduce the power to 70%, cover, and cook for 2 minutes; stir, cover again, and cook at 70% for 2 to 3 minutes longer.
— Drain the cooking liquid, add the lemon juice to the squid and shrimp, and let cool for several hours.
— When the squid and shrimp mixture is

thoroughly chilled, add the cubed avocado and the celery; season to taste.
— Arrange the salad on lettuce leaves.
— Garnish with parsley before serving.

Cover the squid and shrimp pieces with the seasoned onion and garlic mixture.

When the squid and shrimp mixture has completely cooled, add the cubed avocado and the celery.

Clams with Risotto

Level of Difficulty	
Preparation Time	15 min
Cost per Serving	$ $
Number of Servings	4
Nutritional Value	274 calories 18.6 g protein 2.1 g lipids
Food Exchanges	2.5 oz meat 1 bread exchange
Cooking Time	27 min
Standing Time	None
Power Level	90%, 100%, 70%
Write Your Cooking Time Here	

Ingredients
24 clams, washed and scrubbed
500 mL (2 cups) hot chicken stock
1 mL (1/4 teaspoon) saffron
15 mL (1 tablespoon) parsley, chopped
250 mL (1 cup) uncooked rice
10 mL (2 teaspoons) cornstarch
30 mL (2 tablespoons) water
125 mL (1/2 cup) fish stock
salt and pepper to taste

Method
— Place the clams, in their shells, in a circle on a large plate.
— Add 45 mL (3 tablespoons) hot water from the tap; cover and cook at 90% for 4 to 5 minutes, or until the clams open, giving the plate a half-turn halfway through the cooking time.
— Remove and discard any clams that remain unopened.

⟹

Clams with Risotto

Carefully clean and scrub each clam before cooking.

When cooking the rice, give the dish a half-turn halfway through the cooking time to ensure uniform cooking.

Combine the clams, cooked rice and sauce before reheating and serving.

— Remove the clams from their shells and set aside.
— In another dish, combine the chicken stock, saffron and parsley. Stir in the rice, cover, and cook at 100% for 5 minutes; reduce the power to 70% and cook for 10 more minutes, stirring once and giving the dish a half-turn after 5 minutes. Set aside.
— Dissolve the cornstarch in the water and stir into the fish stock; cook at 100% for 2 to 3 minutes, or until the mixture thickens, stirring every minute.

— Combine the clams, the cooked rice and the sauce in a dish and adjust the seasoning.
— Cover and reheat at 70% for 3 to 4 minutes, or until heated through.

MICROTIPS

Ideas for Leftover Seafood

Leftover seafood can be reheated with other ingredients in many interesting ways and attractively served in scallop shells. When using cooked ingredients you only need a few minutes at 70% power to prepare a number of original and inexpensive dishes. Arrange the ingredients in scallop shells, real or porcelain, or use ramekins or any other microwave-safe dishes. Garnish with vegetables or an appropriate sauce. Try some of these ideas for meals in a shell. Combine leftover seafood with:

— mushrooms, lemon juice, and béchamel sauce.
— tomatoes, cooked rice, thyme, and black olives.
— cooked spinach, 35% cream, salt and pepper.
— cooked minced leeks, 35% cream, salt, and pepper.

Scallops on the Half Shell

Ingredients
450 g (1 lb) scallops
90 mL (6 tablespoons) dry white wine
1 small onion, minced

1 bouquet garni
1 clove garlic, crushed
50 mL (1/4 cup) mushrooms, thinly sliced
30 mL (2 tablespoons) butter, melted
60 mL (4 tablespoons) 18% cream
60 mL (4 tablespoons) breadcrumbs
15 mL (1 tablespoon) parsley, chopped
4 scallop shells

Level of Difficulty	🍴🍴
Preparation Time	10 min
Cost per Serving	$ $
Number of Servings	4
Nutritional Value	218 calories 20.9 g protein 9.1 g lipids
Food Exchanges	2.5 oz meat 1 fat exchange
Cooking Time	10 min
Standing Time	2 min
Power Level	70%
Write Your Cooking Time Here	

Method
— Combine the white wine, onion, bouquet garni, garlic and mushrooms.
— Rinse the scallops and add to this mixture.
— Cover and cook at 70% for 5 to 6 minutes, giving the dish a half-turn and stirring halfway through the cooking time.
— Remove the cooked scallop mixture and arrange on each shell.
— Add a little melted butter and cream to each serving, sprinkle with breadcrumbs, and garnish with parsley.
— Reheat at 70% for 3 to 4 minutes.
— Let stand for 2 minutes before serving.

Oysters au Gratin

Level of Difficulty	[cutlery icons]
Preparation Time	20 min
Cost per Serving	$ $
Number of Servings	2
Nutritional Value	281 calories 21.6 g protein 9.7 g lipids
Food Exchanges	3 oz meat 1 fat exchange 1/2 bread exchange
Cooking Time	6 min
Standing Time	2 min
Power Level	90%
Write Your Cooking Time Here	[pencil and apple icon]

Ingredients
12 fresh oysters, washed and scrubbed
125 mL (1/2 cup) sour cream
30 mL (2 tablespoons) lemon juice
115 g (4 oz) clams
salt and pepper to taste
60 mL (4 tablespoons) breadcrumbs
15 mL (1 tablespoon) parsley, chopped

Method
— Open the shells and remove the oysters; drain, and reserve the liquor.
— Strain the liquor through a fine sieve to remove any particles of sand or shell.
— Add the sour cream, lemon juice and the clams to the filtered liquor and season to taste.
— Arrange the oysters in a baking dish and cover with the sauce.
— Sprinkle with the breadcrumbs and garnish with chopped parsley.
— Cook at 90% for 5 to 6 minutes, or until very hot, giving the dish a half-turn halfway through the cooking time.
— Let stand for 2 minutes before serving.

Open the oysters by inserting the blade of the oyster knife between the shells, near the heel.

Strain the liquor to remove any grains of sand or shell. Proceed with the sauce as directed in the recipe.

Cook as directed, giving the dish a half-turn halfway through the cooking time to ensure uniform cooking.

Crab Cantonese Style

Level of Difficulty	
Preparation Time	10 min
Cost per Serving	$ $
Number of Servings	6
Nutritional Value	156 calories 13.26 g protein 9.9 g lipids
Food Exchanges	2 oz meat 1 vegetable exchange
Cooking Time	13 min
Standing Time	None
Power Level	90%, 100%
Write Your Cooking Time Here	

Ingredients
225 g (1/2 lb) crabmeat, cooked
6 eggs
30 mL (2 tablespoons) soy sauce
salt and pepper to taste
2 tomatoes, peeled and coarsely chopped
15 mL (1 tablespoon) oil
1 onion, minced
1 clove garlic, crushed
2 mL (1/2 teaspoon) ground ginger

Method
— Combine the eggs, soy sauce, salt and pepper and beat well; cook at 90% for 5 to 6 minutes, stirring every 2 minutes.
— Add the chopped tomato, mix well, and set aside.
— In another dish combine the oil, onion, garlic and ginger; cook at 100% for 2 to 3 minutes, stirring once during the cooking time.
— Add the crabmeat and cook at 90% for 2 minutes. Stir in the egg and tomato mixture and reheat at 90% for 2 minutes, stirring once lightly.

Cook the mixture of eggs, soy sauce, salt, and pepper, stirring twice in order to ensure uniform cooking.

Add the crabmeat to the cooked garlic and onion mixture and cook at 90% for 2 minutes.

Combine the two mixtures and reheat at 90% for 2 minutes, stirring once lighly.

Crab Florentine Style

Level of Difficulty	🍴🍴
Preparation Time	10 min
Cost per Serving	$ $
Number of Servings	4
Nutritional Value	384 calories 24.8 g protein 26.8 g lipids
Food Exchanges	4 oz meat 2 vegetable exchanges 1 fat exchange
Cooking Time	28 min
Standing Time	5 min
Power Level	100%, 70%
Write Your Cooking Time Here	

Ingredients

225 g (1/2 lb) crabmeat, cooked
1 284 g (10 oz) package of fresh spinach
45 mL (3 tablespoons) butter
2 onions, chopped
6 eggs, beaten
250 mL (1 cup) 10% cream
45 mL (3 tablespoons) dry white wine
pinch of cayenne pepper
50 mL (1/4 cup) mozzarella cheese, finely grated
paprika to garnish

Method

— Rinse the spinach, place in a covered dish, and cook at 100% for 3 to 4 minutes, giving the dish a half-turn halfway through cooking.

— Use a sieve to drain the spinach; dry carefully by squeezing the spinach with the hands, and chop finely.

— Melt the butter in a dish at 100% for 50 to 60 seconds; add the onion and cook at 100% for 2 to 3 minutes.

— Combine the eggs, cream, wine and cayenne. Set aside.

— Add the spinach and crabmeat to the cooked onion.

— Combine this mixture with the egg-based mixture and stir well.

— Pour the resulting mixture into a 20 cm (8 in) round dish and sprinkle with the grated mozzarella cheese and paprika.

— Cover the dish and place it on a rack in the oven; reduce the power to 70% and cook for 17 to 20 minutes, or until cooked, giving the dish a half-turn halfway through the cooking time.

— Let stand, covered, for 5 minutes before serving.

The spinach and mozzarella, combined with the delicate flavor of the crabmeat, give this dish its special flavor.

Crab Florentine Style

Drain the spinach carefully in two steps; use a sieve and a spoon to squeeze the moisture out of the spinach and then dry completely by pressing into a ball with your hands.

Once the spinach, crabmeat, and egg mixture are combined, pour into a 20 cm (8 in) round dish.

Use a rack or an overturned plate to elevate the dish before beginning the last stage of cooking.

MICROTIPS

Some Simple and Inexpensive Ways to Enjoy Crabmeat

Crabmeat is renowned for its delicate, subtle flavor. There are many different ways to enjoy leftover crabmeat. If all the ingredients you need are cooked, all you have to do is reheat them in the microwave oven at 70% for a few minutes. Try the following suggestions with leftover crabmeat, adjusting the seasonings to suit your own particular tastes:

— Crabmeat Bordelaise: Flaked crabmeat with mushrooms in a wine sauce.
— Garnished Crabmeat: Flaked crabmeat seasoned with salt, cayenne, dry mustard, vinegar, and oil or mayonnaise to bind. Spread in a scallop shell and garnish with hard-boiled egg slices, chopped parsley, capers and a lemon slice. Serve cold.
— Crabmeat Indian Style: Flaked crabmeat mixed with a curry sauce and served with cooked white rice.
— Crabmeat Mexican Style: Flaked crabmeat mixed with fried chopped onion, diced green pepper, garlic, dry mustard and Worcestershire sauce, serve in a scallop shell coated with a cheese sauce.

Crabmeat Casserole

Ingredients
225 g (1/2 lb) crabmeat
6 slices bread
8 slices Gruyère cheese
4 eggs

500 mL (2 cups) milk
5 mL (1 teaspoon) sweet mustard
7 mL (1/2 tablespoon) chives
1 mL (1/4 tablespoon)

cayenne pepper
15 mL (1 tablespoon) parsley, chopped
15 mL (1 tablespoon) flour

Level of Difficulty	🍴
Preparation Time	10 min*
Cost per Serving	$ $
Number of Servings	6
Nutritional Value	357 calories 26.8 g protein 20.1 g lipids
Food Exchanges	3 oz meat 1 bread exchange 1/2 milk exchange
Cooking Time	21 min
Standing Time	3 min
Power Level	70%, 50%
Write Your Cooking Time Here	

* This dish must be refrigerated for 2-1/2 hours before cooking.

Method
— Arrange the slices of bread in a large round dish and distribute the Gruyère cheese and crabmeat evenly over the bread.
— Mix the remaining ingredients in a bowl; whisk vigorously and pour over the crabmeat.
— Refrigerate for 1-1/2 hours before cooking.
— Using a rack or overturned plate, elevate the dish, and cook at 70% for 10 minutes, giving the dish a half-turn halfway through the cooking time.
— Reduce the power to 50% and cook for 9 to 11 minutes longer, or until the middle is cooked, giving the dish a half-turn halfway through cooking.
— Let stand for 3 minutes before serving.

Crab Legs with Lemon Sauce

Level of Difficulty	🍴
Preparation Time	10 min
Cost per Serving	$ $ $
Number of Servings	4
Nutritional Value	262 calories 31.1 g protein 11 g lipids
Food Exchanges	4 oz meat 1 fat exchange
Cooking Time	7 min
Standing Time	None
Power Level	100%, 70%
Write Your Cooking Time Here	

Ingredients
675 g (1-1/2 lb) crab legs, cooked
15 mL (1 tablespoon) butter
15 mL (1 tablespoon) flour
125 mL (1/2 cup) chicken stock
125 mL (1/2 cup) 10% cream
1 egg yolk
30 mL (2 tablespoons) lemon juice
15 mL (1 tablespoon) lime juice
salt and pepper to taste
grated lime zest to garnish

Method
— Melt the butter in a dish at 100% for 30 seconds; stir in the flour and mix well.
— Blend in the chicken stock, cream and egg yolk, and cook at 100% for 1 minute.
— Stir, reduce the power to 70% and continue to cook for 1 minute; stir again, and if the sauce is not thick enough, cook for another 30 to 40 seconds.
— Add the lemon juice and the lime juice; season to taste, cover and set aside.
— In another dish, add the crab legs to 75 mL (1/3 cup) of hot tap water; cover and heat through at 70% for 3 to 4 minutes.
— Pour the prepared sauce into 4 ramekins and sprinkle with the lime zest.
— Serve the crab legs accompanied by the sauce.

Assemble all the ingredients needed for this easy-to-make gourmet dish.

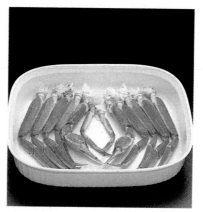

Heat the crab legs in hot water, placing the larger legs toward the outside of the dish.

MICROTIPS

Removing the Meat from the Crab Legs

Use a nut cracker or sharp kitchen shears to crack the shell. The meat is then surprisingly easy to remove with your fingers or with a nut pick.

Crabmeat Salad on Croissants

Level of Difficulty	⑪
Preparation Time	10 min
Cost per Serving	$ $
Number of Servings	4
Nutritional Value	255 calories 14.7 g protein 14.4 g lipids
Food Exchanges	1.5 oz meat 2 fat exchanges 1 bread exchange
Cooking Time	1 min each
Standing Time	None
Power Level	100%
Write Your Cooking Time Here	

Ingredients
175 g (6 oz) crabmeat, cooked
75 mL (1/3 cup) sour cream
30 mL (2 tablespoons) mayonnaise
2 mL (1/2 teaspoon) onion powder
salt and pepper to taste
125 mL (1/2 cup) seedless green grapes, cut in two
125 mL (1/2 cup) celery, chopped
4 croissants
4 leaves Boston lettuce
125 mL (1/2 cup) cheddar cheese, finely grated

Method
— Drain the crabmeat and set aside.
— Combine the sour cream, mayonnaise and onion powder; add salt and pepper to taste and set aside.
— Combine the crabmeat with the grapes and celery.
— Then combine the two mixtures.
— Slice each croissant in two; arrange half a lettuce leaf on each half.
— Spread the crabmeat mixture evenly on each croissant half and sprinkle with cheddar cheese.
— Heat each croissant individually at 100% for 1 minute and serve at once.

Assemble the ingredients needed to make this delicious dish—ideal for a tasty snack or a quick supper.

Drain the crabmeat before mixing it with the grapes and celery.

Spread the final crabmeat mixture on the open face croissants and sprinkle with cheddar cheese before placing in the microwave oven.

Steamed Clams with Garlic Butter

Level of Difficulty	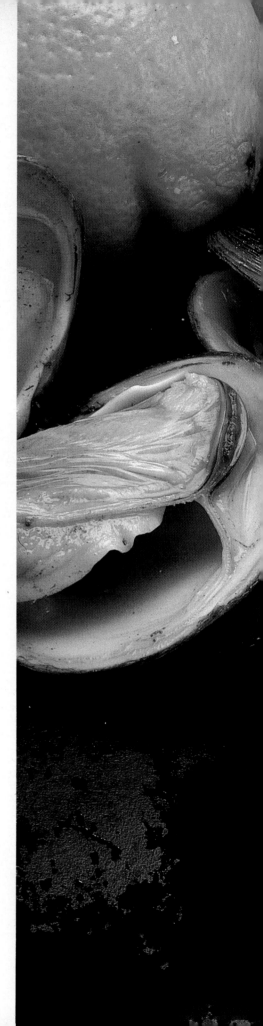
Preparation Time	10 min
Cost per Serving	$ $
Number of Servings	2
Nutritional Value	571 calories 28 g protein 47.8 g lipids
Food Exchanges	4 oz meat 6 fat exchanges
Cooking Time	13 min
Standing Time	None
Power Level	100%, 90%
Write Your Cooking Time Here	

Ingredients
24 clams
125 mL (1/2 cup) butter
3 cloves garlic, curshed
30 mL (2 tablespoons) fresh parsley, chopped
5 mL (1 teaspoon) lemon juice

Method
— Carefully wash and scrub the clams.
— Arrange 12 calms on a plate, cover, and cook at 90% for 4 to 5 minutes, or until the shells open.
— Remove and discard any unopened shells and set the plate aside.
— Repeat the operation with the other 12 clams.

— Mix the butter, garlic, parsley and lemon juice in small bowl.
— Cook at 100% for 2 to 3 minutes.
— Serve the clams and the garlic butter separately.

Steamed Clams Oriental Style

Level of Difficulty	🍴🔪
Preparation Time	10 min
Cost per Serving	💲 💲
Number of Servings	2
Nutritional Value	316 calories 28 g protein 20.3 g lipids
Food Exchanges	4 oz meat 1 fat exchange
Cooking Time	10 min (+ 2 min per serving)
Standing Time	None
Power Level	90%, 100%
Write Your Cooking Time Here	✏️🍎

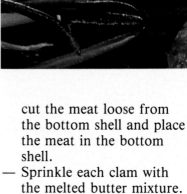

Ingredients
24 clams
125 mL (1/2 cup) butter
3 cloves garlic, crushed
30 mL (2 tablespoons) fresh parsley, chopped
5 mL (1 teaspoon) lemon juice
5 mL (1 teaspoon) lemon zest, grated
5 mL (1 teaspoon) ground ginger

Method
— Arrange 12 clams in a dish, cover and cook at 90% for 4 to 5 minutes, or until the shells open.
— Remove and discard any unopened shells.
— Repeat the operation with the other 12 clams.
— Melt the butter in a dish at 100% for 40 seconds, add the remaining ingredients, and mix well.
— Remove the top shell of each clam; use a knife to cut the meat loose from the bottom shell and place the meat in the bottom shell.
— Sprinkle each clam with the melted butter mixture.
— Heat 12 clams at 100% for 1 to 2 minutes, or until heated through.
— Repeat the operation with the other 12 clams. Serve.

Assemble the ingredients needed for this delicious, easy-to-make dish.

Arrange 12 clams in a circle in a dish. Cook as directed in the recipe.

Remove and discard any unopened shells; they are not edible.

Clams Portuguese Style

Level of Difficulty	🍴
Preparation Time	10 min
Cost per Serving	$ $
Number of Servings	4
Nutritional Value	425 calories 63.6 g protein 8.6 g lipids
Food Exchanges	5.5 oz meat
Cooking Time	20 min
Standing Time	None
Power Level	100%, 70%
Write Your Cooking Time Here	✏️

Ingredients
1.8 kg (4 lb) clams
5 cloves garlic, finely
chopped
1 bay leaf, crushed
250 mL (1 cup) white wine

Method
— Immerse a clay baker in
  ice water to cool.
— Carefully wash and brush
  the clams; remove the clay
  baker from the water and
  arrange the clams in it.
— Add all the other
  ingredients, cover, and
  cook at 100% for 5
  minutes.
— Stir, reduce the power to
  70%, cover, and continue
  to cook for 10 to 15
  minutes, stirring halfway
  through the cooking time.

*Clams, garlic, a bay leaf,
pepper, and white wine are the
only ingredients necessary to
prepare this recipe.*

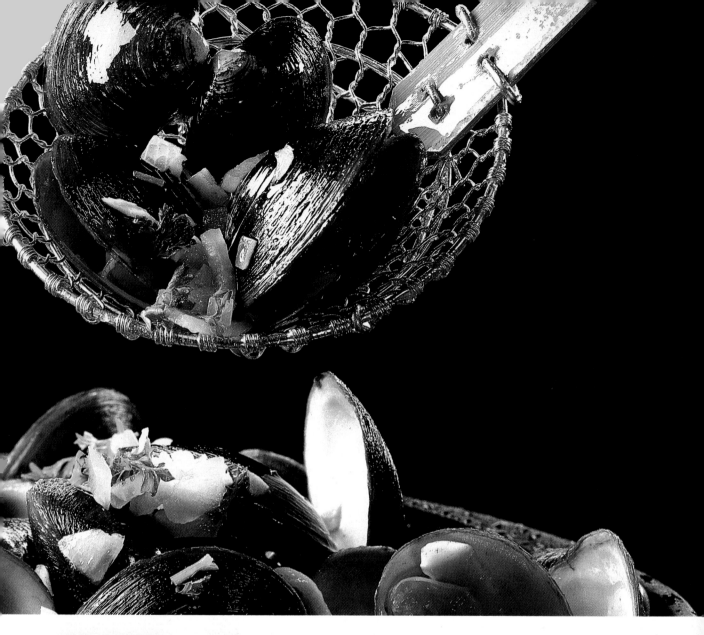

Carefully wash and scrub each clam with a brush before beginning this recipe.

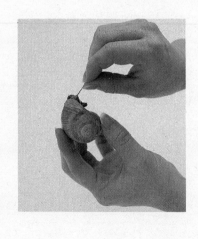

MICROTIPS

To Extract Periwinkles, Whelks or Snails from Their Shells

After cooking these mollusks, prick the meat with a needle and pull it out. Make sure to first remove the small brown membrane covering the openings of periwinkle and whelk shells.

Frogs' Legs Provençale

Level of Difficulty	🍴🍴
Preparation Time	20 min*
Cost per Serving	$ $
Number of Servings	4
Nutritional Value	475 calories 37.6 g protein 24.8 g lipids
Food Exchanges	4.5 oz meat 3 fat exchanges
Cooking Time	20 min
Standing Time	5 min
Power Level	100%, 70%
Write Your Cooking Time Here	

* The frogs' legs should be marinated in the oil and garlic for 4 to 6 hours before preparing this recipe.

Ingredients
900 g (2 lb) frogs' legs, uncooked
500 mL (2 cups) oil
10 cloves garlic, cut in half
125 mL (1/2 cup) butter
50 mL (1/4 cup) fresh parsley, finely chopped
30 mL (2 tablespoons) lemon juice

Method
— Marinate the frogs' legs for 4 to 6 hours in the oil and garlic, stirring occasionally.
— Drain the frogs' legs; place with small ends crossed and prick the flesh close to the bone.
— Arrange the frogs' legs in a round dish, placing the fleshier parts so that they face the outer edge.
— In another dish, melt the butter with the garlic from the marinade at 100% for 2 minutes, stirring after 1 minute. Add the chopped parsley and lemon juice.
— Cook at 100% for 2 minutes, stirring after 1 minute.
— Pour the melted butter over the frogs' legs, reduce the power to 70%, and cook for 7 minutes, turning the frogs' legs over halfway through the cooking time.
— Continue to cook at 70% for 8 to 9 minutes, or until cooked.
— Let stand for 5 minutes before serving.

Assemble the ingredients needed for this dish, one that all your guests are sure to enjoy.

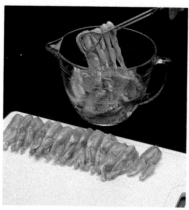

Marinate the frogs' legs for 4 to 6 hours in the oil and garlic before beginning the recipe.

Arrange the frogs' legs in a round dish, placing the fleshier parts toward the outside.

Clams au Gratin

Level of Difficulty	🍴
Preparation Time	10 min
Cost per Serving	$ $
Number of Servings	4
Nutritional Value	403 calories 28.1 g protein 28.4 g lipids
Food Exchanges	4 oz meat 1 vegetable exchange 2 fat exchanges
Cooking Time	10 min (+ 2 min per serving)
Standing Time	None
Power Level	90%, 100%, 70%
Write Your Cooking Time Here	

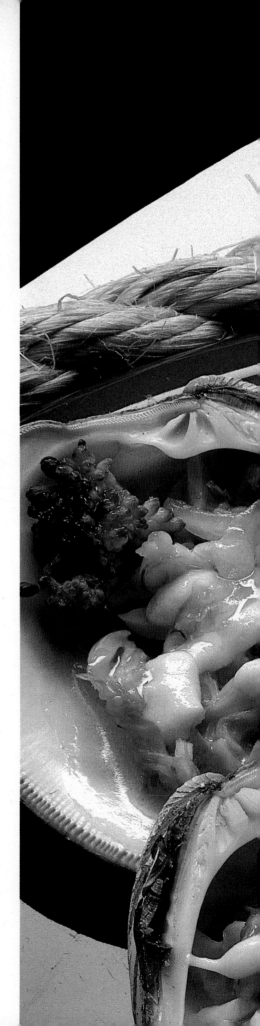

Ingredients
36 clams, washed and scrubbed
500 mL (2 cups) broccoli flowerets, cooked
15 mL (1 tablespoon) butter
1 clove garlic, crushed
1 onion, grated
250 mL (1 cup) 35% cream
125 mL (1/2 cup) Gruyère cheese, grated
salt and pepper to taste
paprika to garnish

Method
— Place the clams in a dish, cover, and cook at 90% for 4 to 5 minutes.
— Pry the shells apart and leave the meat in the bottom shell.
— Place 1 or 2 broccoli flowerets on each clam. Set aside.
— In another dish combine the butter, garlic and onion, and cook at 100% for 1-1/2 minutes.
— Add the cream and 50 mL (1/4 cup) of the Gruyère cheese; season to taste and cook at 90% for 4 minutes.
— Pour the sauce over the clams and sprinkle with the remainder of the cheese and the paprika.
— Arrange the clams on 4 plates and heat each plate individually at 70% for 1 to 2 minutes, or until heated through.

Seafood Kebabs

Level of Difficulty	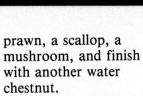
Preparation Time	15 min
Cost per Serving	$ $ $
Number of Servings	4
Nutritional Value	195 calories 19.8 g protein 4.9 g lipids
Food Exchanges	2.5 oz meat 1 vegetable exchange
Cooking Time	10 min
Standing Time	2 min
Power Level	100%, 90%
Write Your Cooking Time Here	

Ingredients
4 bacon slices
4 shrimps
4 prawns
4 scallops
8 water chestnuts
1/2 red pepper, cut into 4 pieces
4 large mushrooms
4 wooden skewers

Honey Sauce:
30 mL (2 tablespoons) honey
30 mL (2 tablespoons) soy sauce
30 mL (2 tablespoons) white wine
1 mL (1/4 teaspoon) ground ginger
1 mL (1/4 teaspoon) garlic powder

Method
— Cut the bacon slices in two, place on a plate, cover with paper towel, and cook at 100% for 2 minutes.
— Shell and devein the shrimps and the prawns and clean the scallops. Drain the water chestnuts.
— Wrap each water chestnut in a piece of bacon and set aside.
— In a bowl, blend all the ingredients for the honey sauce and cook at 100% for 1-1/2 to 2 minutes.
— On each wooden skewer thread a water chestnut wrapped in bacon, a piece of red pepper, a shrimp, a prawn, a scallop, a mushroom, and finish with another water chestnut.
— Brush each skewer with the honey sauce and place over a dish, the ends of the skewers balancing on the edges of the dish.
— Cover and cook at 90% for 3 minutes, moving the center skewers to the ends of the dish and the outside skewers to the center halfway through the cooking time.
— Continue to cook for 2 to

3 minutes, or until the
seafood is cooked.
— Let stand uncovered for 2
minutes before serving.

*Arrange the skewers on a
microwave-safe dish, the ends
balancing on the rim of the
dish.*

*To ensure uniform cooking,
alternate the position of the
skewers halfway through the
cooking time.*

Oysters Sautéed with Mushrooms

Level of Difficulty	
Preparation Time	10 min
Cost per Serving	$ $
Number of Servings	2
Nutritional Value	533 calories 46.9 g protein 20.6 g lipids
Food Exchanges	5 oz meat 1 vegetable exchange 2 fat exchanges 1/2 bread exchange
Cooking Time	10 min (+ 1-1/2 min per serving)
Standing Time	2 min
Power Level	100%, 90%, 70%
Write Your Cooking Time Here	

Ingredients
900 g (2 lb) small oysters
30 mL (2 tablespoons) butter
225 g (8 oz) mushrooms, sliced
50 mL (1/4 cup) white wine
15 mL (1 tablespoon) dried parsley
salt and pepper to taste
30 mL (2 tablespoons) breadcrumbs

Method
— Shell the oysters and rinse under cold running water; arrange in a dish.

— Melt half the butter at 100% for 30 seconds and add it to the oysters.
— Cover and cook at 70% for 2 minutes and then move the oysters from the center of the dish to the edges.
— Continue to cook at 70% for 1 to 2 minutes more, or until the edges of the oysters turn up slightly.
— Let stand covered for 2 minutes and set aside.
— In another dish melt the remainder of the butter at 100% for 30 seconds; add

the mushrooms, cover, and cook at 100% for 2 to 3 minutes.
— Stir in the white wine and the parsley and season to taste.
— Cover and cook at 100% for 1 to 1-1/2 minutes, or until very hot.
— Divide the oysters into two au gratin dishes and cover with equal amounts of the cooked mushrooms

and wine.
— Sprinkle with breadcrumbs
  and heat each plate
  individually at 90% for 1
  to 1-1/2 minutes.

MICROTIPS

A Delicious Mix of Flavors

When it comes to seafood, an infinite number of taste combinations are possible. Here are just a few suggestions for pairing particular seafoods with foods that complement them especially well:

— salmon and grapefruit
— sole and salsify (oyster plant)
— cod and tomato
— halibut and spinach
— haddock and green peas
— plaice and asparagus
— pike and almonds
— lobster and prunes
— shrimp and avocado
— herring and onions

Seafood Vol-au-Vents

Level of Difficulty	🍴
Preparation Time	10 min
Cost per Serving	$ $
Number of Servings	8
Nutritional Value*	625 calories 36.8 g protein 33.3 g lipids
Food Exchanges	4.5 oz meat 3 fat exchanges 1 bread exchange 1/2 milk exchange
Cooking Time	19 min
Standing Time	None
Power Level	100%, 70%
Write Your Cooking Time Here	

Ingredients
450 g (1 lb) scallops, rinsed
450 g (1 lb) shrimps, shelled and deveined
175 mL (3/4 cup) butter
175 mL (3/4 cup) flour
750 mL (3 cups) milk
340 g (12 oz) Gruyère cheese, grated
1 mL (1/4 teaspoon) garlic powder
salt and pepper to taste
1 mL (1/4 teaspoon) dry mustard
5 mL (1 teaspoon) tomato paste
15 mL (3 teaspoons) lemon juice
225 g (8 oz) mushrooms
8 ramekins or puff pastry shells

Method
— Melt the butter at 100% for 1 minute, add the flour, and mix well.
— Stir in the milk and cook at 100% for 7 to 8 minutes, or until the mixture thickens, stirring every 2 minutes.
— Add the Gruyère cheese stirring well.
— Add the garlic powder, salt, pepper, dry mustard, tomato paste, and 10 mL (2 teaspoons) of the lemon juice. Mix well and set aside.
— Place the mushrooms in another dish, cover, and cook at 100% for 3 to 4 minutes, stirring once during the cooking time.
— Drain the mushrooms, add them to the sauce, and set aside.
— Place the scallops and shrimps in another dish, add 15 mL (1 tablespoon) water and the remaining lemon juice, reduce the power to 70%, cover, and cook for 4 to 5 minutes, stirring halfway through the cooking time.
— Remove the cooked shrimps and scallops and add them to the sauce. If the sauce is too thick, add

the liquid from the cooked seafood and, if necessary, a little milk. Reheat the sauce.

— Set the ramekins or pastry shells on paper towel and heat at 70% for 60 to 90 seconds. Fill with the sauce and serve.

Add the Gruyère cheese to the heated sauce, stirring well to melt the cheese.

Once the seafood is cooked, add it to the prepared sauce.

Spaghettini with Seafood

Ingredients
250 mL (1 cup) shrimps, shelled and deveined
1 213 mL (7-1/2 oz) can crabmeat
250 mL (1 cup) lobster meat, cooked
1 284 mL (10 oz) can cream of tomato soup
250 mL (1 cup) 35% cream
lemon juice to taste
salt and pepper to taste
115 g (1/4 lb) spaghettini, cooked al dente
45 mL (3 tablespoons) chives

Method
— Arrange the shrimps in a dish, placing the fleshy parts toward the outer edge.
— Cover and cook at 70% for 2 to 3 minutes, stirring halfway through the cooking time.
— Drain the cooking juices and set the shrimps aside.
— Combine the tomato soup and the 35% cream and heat at 70% for 2 to 3 minutes.

— Add the cooked crabmeat, lobster meat, cooked shrimps and lemon juice; season to taste.
— Place the spaghettini in a dish, cover with the seafood sauce, and sprinkle with chives.
— Cover and cook at 70% for 4 to 5 minutes, or until well heated through, giving the dish a half-turn after 3 minutes.

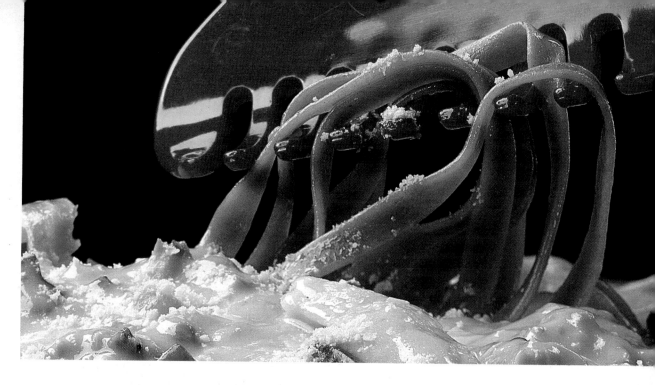

Fettuccine with Seafood

Ingredients

450 g (1 lb) white fish fillets
150 g (5 oz) clams, cooked
225 g (8 oz) small scallops, cooked
30 mL (2 tablespoons) butter
125 mL (1/2 cup) onion, chopped
1 clove garlic, chopped
350 g (12 oz) spinach fettuccine, cooked al dente
salt and pepper to taste
2 284 mL (10 oz) cans of cream of celery soup
125 mL (1/2 cup) milk
30 mL (2 tablespoons) roasted red peppers, chopped
50 mL (1/4 cup) Parmesan cheese, grated

Method

— Melt the butter at 100% for 40 seconds; add the onion and garlic, and cook at 100% for 2 minutes.
— Add the fish fillets, cover, and cook at 90% for 2 minutes; give the dish a half-turn and continue to cook for 2 minutes more, or until the fish is cooked.
— Place the fettuccine in a dish, cover with the fish fillet mixture, season to taste, and set aside.
— Mix the 2 cans of cream of celery soup with the milk, red pepper, clams and scallops and cook at 100% for 3 to 4 minutes, stirring once halfway through the cooking time.
— Cover the fish fillets and fettuccine with the clam and scallop sauce and sprinkle with Parmesan cheese.
— Reduce the power to 70% and cook for 6 to 8 minutes, giving the dish a half-turn halfway through the cooking time.
— Let stand for 4 minutes before serving.

Escargots with Garlic and Green Onion

Level of Difficulty	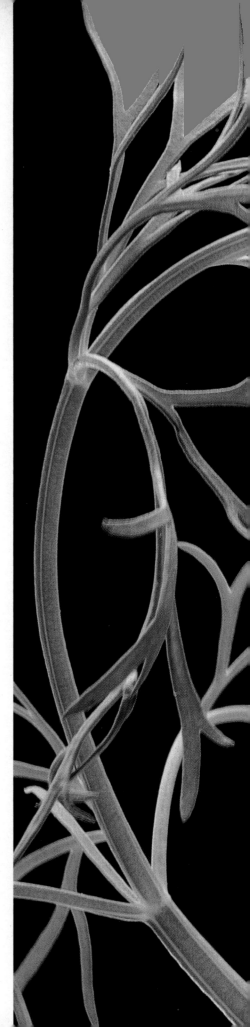 (cutlery icon)
Preparation Time	5 min
Cost per Serving	$
Number of Servings	4
Nutritional Value	294 calories 16.25 g protein 23.4 g lipids
Food Exchanges	2 oz meat 3 fat exchanges
Cooking Time	7 min
Standing Time	2 min
Power Level	30%, 50%
Write Your Cooking Time Here	

Ingredients
24 escargots
125 mL (1/2 cup) butter
45 mL (3 tablespoons) green onion, finely chopped
2 cloves garlic, finely chopped
white pepper to taste
15 mL (1 tablespoon) dried parsley
5 mL (1 teaspoon) lemon juice

Method
— Soften the butter at 30% for 1 minute; add all the other ingredients except the escargots and mix well.
— Arrange the escargots in 4 microwave-safe dishes and top with the butter mixture.
— Cover and cook at 50% for 5 to 6 minutes, giving each dish a half-turn halfway through the cooking time.
— Let stand for 2 minutes before serving.

Squid Stuffed with Ham

Level of Difficulty	🍴🍴🍴
Preparation Time	1 h
Cost per Serving	$ $ $
Number of Servings	4
Nutritional Value	462 calories 55.9 g protein 11.3 g lipids
Food Exchanges	4.5 oz meat 2 vegetable exchanges 1 bread exchange
Cooking Time	8 min
Standing Time	3 min
Power Level	100%, 70%
Write Your Cooking Time Here	

Ingredients
900 g (2 lb) squids, of equal size
125 mL (1/2 cup) stale bread
50 mL (1/4 cup) milk
200 g (7 oz) cooked ham, coarsely chopped
2 cloves garlic, chopped
4 sprigs parsley, chopped
2 eggs
salt and pepper to taste
30 mL (2 tablespoons) oil
50 mL (1/4 cup) onion, grated
175 mL (6 oz) tomatoes, drained, peeled, and crushed
50 mL (1/4 cup) white wine

Method
— Clean the squid, removing the ink sac and spine.
— Cut off the head and tentacles and chop the tentacles into small pieces.
— Crumble the bread, moisten it in the milk, and combine the chopped tentacles, bread, ham, garlic and parsley.
— Stir in the eggs, mix well, and season to taste.
— Fill each squid with a moderate amount of stuffing; secure with a toothpick, and set aside.
— Preheat a browning dish at 100% for 7 minutes.
— Add the oil, heat for 30 seconds, and sear the squid in the oil.
— Add the onion, tomatoes and white wine; cover and cook at 70% for 5 to 7 minutes, stirring halfway through the cooking time.
— Let stand for 3 minutes before serving.

Clean and trim the squid. Remove the head and the tentacles.

Use a piping bag to stuff the squid.

MICROTIPS

To Reheat Coffee

You can reheat coffee quickly in a microwave oven without losing any of its original good flavor. Simply place the cup in the middle of the oven and heat at 100% for 1 minute.

Seafood Casserole

Level of Difficulty	
Preparation Time	15 min
Cost per Serving	$ $
Number of Servings	4
Nutritional Value	192 calories 25.3 g protein 6.1 g lipids
Food Exchanges	3 oz meat 1 vegetable exchange
Cooking Time	12 min
Standing Time	2 min
Power Level	100%, 70%
Write Your Cooking Time Here	

Ingredients
225 g (1/2 lb) fresh shrimps
340 g (3/4 lb) scallops
30 mL (2 tablespoons) butter
125 mL (1/2 cup) onion, finely chopped
2 cloves garlic, crushed
1/2 green pepper, cut into strips
1/2 red pepper, cut into strips
1/2 yellow pepper, cut into strips
125 mL (1/2 cup) tomatoes, drained, peeled and crushed
2 mL (1/2 teaspoon) curry powder
5 mL (1 teaspoon) paprika
2 mL (1/2 teaspoon) sugar
50 mL (1/4 cup) fish stock

Method
— Melt the butter at 100% for 40 seconds; add the onion, garlic and peppers.
— Cover and cook at 100% for 2 to 3 minutes, stirring once halfway through the cooking time.
— Add the tomatoes, curry powder, paprika and sugar and mix well.
— Cover and cook at 100% for 1-1/2 minutes; set aside.
— Shell and devein the shrimps; trim the scallops and slice in two.
— Add the shrimps, scallops and fish stock to the tomatoes and peppers.
— Cover and cook at 70% for 3 minutes; stir and cook for 3 to 4 minutes longer, or until the seafood is done.
— Let stand for 2 minutes before serving.

Assemble all the ingredients needed for this dish, one that is guaranteed to please the most fastidious taste.

Shell and devein the shrimps, trim the scallops and slice them in two.

Combine the seafood with the tomato and pepper mixture. Cook at 70% for 6 to 7 minutes, stirring halfway through the cooking time.

Seafood Quiche

Level of Difficulty	
Preparation Time	10 min
Cost per Serving	$ $ $
Number of Servings	4
Nutritional Value	486 calories 22.5 g protein 35.9 g lipids
Food Exchanges	3.5 oz meat 3 fat exchanges 1 bread exchange
Cooking Time	13 min
Standing Time	3 min
Power Level	100%, 70%
Write Your Cooking Time Here	

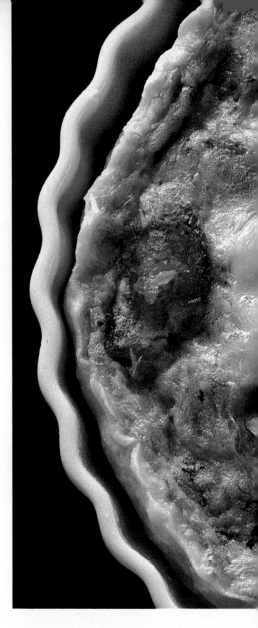

Ingredients
150 g (5 oz) lobster meat, cooked
150 g (5 oz) crabmeat, cooked
30 mL (2 tablespoons) butter
3 green onions, chopped
30 mL (2 tablespoons) fresh parsley, chopped
2 mL (1/2 teaspoon) salt
2 mL (1/2 teaspoon) pepper
30 mL (2 tablespoons) dry vermouth
3 eggs, beaten
250 mL (1 cup) 18% cream
15 mL (1 tablespoon) tomato paste
1 pie shell, 22.5 cm (9 in) diameter, baked
50 mL (1/4 cup) Gruyère cheese, grated
paprika to garnish

Method
— Melt the butter at 100% for 45 seconds and add the green onion and parsley.
— Cook at 100% for 1-1/2 to 2 minutes, add the lobster and crabmeat, and season to taste.
— Add the vermouth, cover, and cook at 100% for 2 minutes; set aside.
— Combine the cream and tomato paste with the eggs, beating vigorously.
— Add the lobster and crabmeat mixture to the custard base and adjust the seasoning.
— Pour the mixture into the pie shell.
— Sprinkle with the Gruyère cheese and paprika.
— Place the dish on a rack and cook at 70% for 7 to 8 minutes, turning halfway through the cooking time.
— Cover and let stand for 3 minutes before serving.

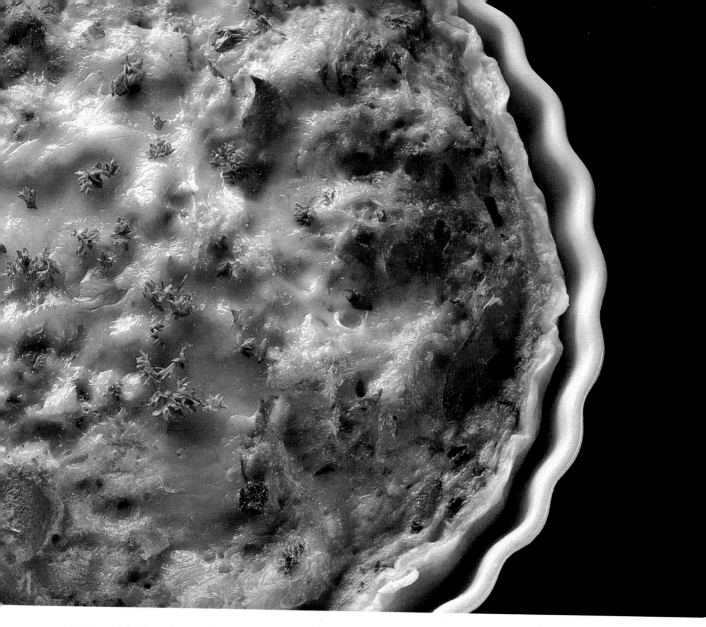

Assemble all the ingredients needed for this savory, easy-to-prepare dish.

Add the cream and tomato paste to the beaten eggs, beating vigorously.

Place the dish on a rack and cook at 70% for 7 to 8 minutes, giving the dish a half-turn halfway through the cooking time.

Seafood Hors d'Oeuvres

Level of Difficulty	🍴
Preparation Time	10 min
Cost per Serving	$ $
Number of Servings	8
Nutritional Value*	316 calories 40.7 g protein 15.4 g lipids
Food Exchanges	4 oz meat 2 fat exchanges
Cooking Time	9 min
Standing Time	None
Power Level	90%, 100%
Write Your Cooking Time Here	🍎✏️

* Amounts given do not include the use of pastry shells.

Ingredients
450 g (1 lb) haddock fillets
340 g (12 oz) crabmeat, cooked
1 can flat anchovy fillets
60 mL (4 tablespoons) butter
30 mL (2 tablespoons) fresh parsley, chopped
salt and pepper to taste

Method
— Arrange the haddock in a dish and cook at 90% for 4 to 5 minutes, giving the dish a half-turn halfway through the cooking time.

— Drain and discard the cooking juices. Cut the haddock fillets into small slices.
— Add the crabmeat to the haddock and mix well.
— Stir in the anchovies, butter and parsley and season.
— Increase the power to 100% and cook for 2 minutes; stir, and continue to cook for another 2 minutes.
— Let cool and serve in small coquilles or pastry shells.

Assemble all the ingredients needed for this delicious hors d'oeuvre.

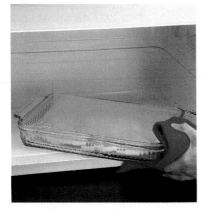

Cook the haddock at 90% for 4 to 5 minutes, giving the dish a half-turn halfway through the cooking time.

Add the crabmeat and the other ingredients to the cooked haddock. Cook at 100% for 4 minutes, stirring halfway through the cooking time.

MICROTIPS

Quick Garlic Butter

The flavor of garlic butter complements almost every type of shellfish. To prepare garlic butter in the microwave, simply crush 3 cloves of garlic, mix with 250 mL (1 cup) of butter, and heat at 100% for 1 to 2 minutes. The garlic butter can be stored in the refrigerator for several weeks.

Coquilles Saint-Jacques

Level of Difficulty	🍴🍴
Preparation Time	10 min
Cost per Serving	$ $
Number of Servings	4
Nutritional Value	390 calories 26.7 g protein 18.2 g lipids
Food Exchanges	2.5 oz meat 1 vegetable exchange 1/4 milk exchange 1 bread exchange 1-1/2 fat exchanges
Cooking Time	14 min
Standing Time	2 min
Power Level	70%, 100%
Write Your Cooking Time Here	

Ingredients
450 g (1 lb) scallops
50 mL (1/4 cup) dry white wine
30 mL (2 tablespoons) butter
15 mL (1 tablespoon) green onions, chopped
30 mL (2 tablespoons) flour
white pepper to taste
175 mL (3/4 cup) milk or light cream
125 mL (1/2 cup) mushrooms, sliced
75 mL (1/3 cup) Swiss cheese, grated
50 mL (1/4 cup) breadcrumbs
parsley, chopped
500 mL (2 cups) potatoes, mashed

Method
— Place the scallops in a dish and sprinkle with the wine.
— Cover and cook at 70% for 5 to 6 minutes, stirring once after 3 minutes.
— Drain, reserving 50 mL (1/4 cup) of the cooking juices. Set the scallops aside.
— Cook the butter and green onions at 100% for 1 minute; add the flour and pepper, and mix well.
— Blend in the milk or cream and the cooking liquid and mix well.
— Reduce the power to 70% and cook for 3 to 4 minutes, stirring twice during the cooking time.
— Add the cooked scallops, mushrooms and cheese; pour the mixture into 4 scallop shells and arrange the mashed potatoes decoratively around it.
— Sprinkle with the breadcrumbs and parsley and cook at 70% for 2 to 3 minutes, or until the mixture is heated through.
— Let stand for 2 minutes before serving.

As the scallops cook, stir
halfway through the cooking
time.

Drain the cooked scallops and
reserve 50 mL (1/4 cup) of the
cooking liquid.

Sprinkle the finished dish with
breadcrumbs and parsley
before the final stage of
cooking.

Paella

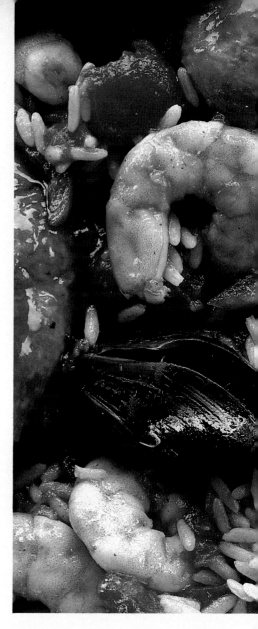

Level of Difficulty	🍴
Preparation Time	20 min
Cost per Serving	$ $
Number of Servings	8
Nutritional Value	310 calories 27 g protein 6.2 g lipids
Food Exchanges	3 oz meat 1 vegetable exchange 1 fat exchange 1 bread exchange
Cooking Time	26 min
Standing Time	5 min
Power Level	100%, 90%, 70%
Write Your Cooking Time Here	

Ingredients
4 chicken wings
4 chicken drumsticks
450 g (1 lb) shrimps, shelled and deveined
12 mussels, washed and scrubbed
45 mL (3 tablespoons) oil
1 green pepper, cut into strips
2 cloves garlic, crushed
1 796 mL (28 oz) can tomatoes, with their liquid
175 mL (3/4 cup) hot water
375 mL (1-1/2 cups) rice
2 mL (1/2 teaspoon) cinnamon
salt and pepper to taste
5 mL (1 teaspoon) sugar
1 340 g (12 oz) package frozen peas
300 mL (2 tablespoons) roasted red pepper, chopped

Method
— Preheat a browning dish at 100% for 7 minutes; add the oil, and heat at 100% for 30 seconds.
— Sear the chicken wings and drumsticks; add the green pepper strips and garlic.
— Cook at 100%, cover, and cook for 2 minutes; stir and continue to cook at 100% for another 2 minutes.
— Add the tomatoes (with their liquid), hot water, rice, cinnamon, salt, pepper and sugar.
— Cover and cook at 90% for 10 to 12 minutes, stirring halfway through the cooking time.

— Pour the mixture into a large casserole dish. Add the peas, red peppers and shrimps and mix well.
— Distribute the mussels over the top, reduce the power to 70%, cover, and cook for 5 to 10 minutes, or until the rice is done and the mussel shells are open and the liquid has evaporated. Give the dish a half-turn halfway through the cooking time.
— Let stand for 5 minutes before serving.

Sear the chicken wings and drumsticks in the browning dish, preheated at 100% for 7 minutes.

Transfer the chicken and tomato mixture to a large casserole dish and add the shrimps, peas, and red pepper.

Place the mussels around the top of the dish before proceeding with the last stage of cooking.

Entertaining

Menu:
Tomato Sorbet
Cream of Celery Soup
Captain's Plate
Crème Royale

With a microwave oven in the kitchen there is no need to wait for an extra special occasion to prepare an elegant dinner for your family or friends. As the main course for such a dinner, we suggest the above menu, featuring the Captain's Plate, a *pièce de resistance* to delight your guests.

The Captain's Plate is definitely one of the seafood lover's favorite dishes. Composed of frogs' legs, shrimps, scallops, prawns, lobster claws and mussels, it is a true feast.

The meal begins with a tomato sorbet, a light appetizer to pique the palates of your guests. We suggest that the sorbet be followed by a smooth tasting cream of celery soup and, for dessert, a crème royale, to conclude this sumptuous meal on a fresh note.

From the Recipe to Your Table

Good planning will ensure that a meal with friends or family does not become a problem or a chore. It goes without saying that an entire meal prepared in a microwave oven should be organized, in the same way as if you were using a traditional oven. Only the cooking and reheating times vary.

24 hours before the meal:
—Prepare the tomato sorbet and the crème royale.
2 hours before the meal:
—Prepare the Captain's Plate.
1 hour before the meal:
—Prepare the cream of celery soup.
15 minutes before the meal:
—Reheat the cream of celery soup.
10 minutes before the meal:
—Reheat each serving of the Captain's Plate.

Tomato Sorbet

Ingredients
250 mL (1 cup) tomato juice
75 mL (1/3 cup) vodka
juice of 1 lemon
4 drops of Worcestershire
sauce
4 ice cubes, crushed
4 celery leaves, finely
chopped
pinch celery salt
pinch pepper
4 sprigs watercress to garnish

Method
— Pour the tomato juice,
vodka, lemon juice,
Worcestershire sauce, and
crushed ice into a blender
and mix at top speed for 1
minute, until the ice
melts.
— Add the celery leaves,
celery salt and pepper and
blend well.
— Pour this mixture into a
large bowl and place in
the freezer for 1 to 2
hours, or until the edges
of the sorbet appear to be
frozen.

— Remove the bowl from
the freezer, whip the
sorbet with a whisk, and
return it to the freezer,
leaving it there for 2 to 3
hours.
— About 30 minutes before
serving, move the bowl to
the refrigerator.
— Spoon equal quantities of
the sorbet into 4 serving
bowls. Wash the
watercress and use to
garnish the sorbets.

Cream of Celery Soup

Ingredients
1 bunch celery
30 mL (2 tablespoons) butter
2 medium onions, chopped
1.125 L (4-1/2 cups) hot
chicken stock
pepper to taste
115 g (4 oz) blue cheese
125 mL (1/2 cup) 35% cream
2 egg yolks

Method
— Wash the celery, remove
the leaves and set aside,
and cut the stalks into
fine slices.
— Melt the butter in a dish
at 100% for 40 seconds
and add the celery, celery
leaves and onion; cover
and cook at 100% for 4
to 6 minutes, or until the
celery is cooked, stirring
once during the cooking
time.
— Add the hot chicken stock
and the pepper; cover,
and bring to the boil at
100% for 6 to 7 minutes,
stirring once during the
cooking time.
— Pour the soup into a
blender and blend until a
smooth, uniform
consistency is achieved;

pour through a sieve to
remove any remaining
celery filaments. Set aside.
— Crumble the cheese, place
in a small bowl, and heat
at 50% for 40 seconds to
soften.
— Combine the cream and
egg yolks, beating
vigorously.
— Add the softened blue
cheese a bit at a time to
the cream and egg yolk
mixture, mix well, then
beat in 30 mL (2
tablespoons) of the warm
soup with a wire whisk.
— Combine with the soup,
mixing well.
— Cook at 70% for 5 to 7
minutes, stirring every
minute. Do not allow the
soup to boil.

Captain's Plate

Level of Difficulty	🍴🍴
Preparation Time	45 min
Cost per Serving	$ $ $
Number of Servings	4
Nutritional Value	without garlic butter: 441 calories 65.2 g protein 6 g lipids with garlic butter: 845 calories 65.7 g protein 51.8 g lipids
Food Exchanges	5 oz meat 1 bread exchange 5 oz meat 1 bread exchange 9 fat exchanges
Cooking Time	50 min (+ 4 min per serving)
Standing Time	None
Power Level	100%, 70%, 50%
Write Your Cooking Time Here	

Ingredients

8 frogs' legs
8 jumbo shrimps, shelled and deveined
8 scallops
12 mussels
8 prawns
4 lobster claws
250 mL (1 cup) oil
6 cloves garlic, crushed
225 g (1/2 lb) butter
30 mL (2 tablespoons) parsley, chopped
5 mL (1 teaspoon) lemon juice
125 mL (1/2 cup) rice
250 mL (1 cup) hot water
125 mL (1/2 cup) water
45 mL (3 tablespoons) breadcrumbs

Method

— Marinate the frogs' legs for 1 hour in the mixture of oil and garlic; remove the garlic after marinating.
— Prepare the garlic butter: place the butter and garlic in a dish and heat at 100% for 3 to 4 minutes; add the parsley and lemon juice, and set aside.
— Pour the rice and 250 mL (1 cup) hot water into a bowl; cover and cook at 100% for 3 minutes; reduce the power to 70%, and cook for another 7 minutes.
— Add 30 mL (2 tablespoons) of the garlic butter to the cooked rice and set aside.
— Arrange the shrimps and scallops in another dish, cover and cook at 70% for 2 minutes; give the plate a half-turn and cook for 2 minutes longer. Drain the cooking juices, cover, and set aside.
— Pour 125 mL (1/2 cup) water into another dish, add the mussels, cover and cook at 100% for 4 to 5 minutes; remove and discard any unopened shells, and set the mussels aside.
— Prepare the prawns and arrange on a plate; cover and cook at 70% for 5 to 6 minutes, or until completely cooked, giving the plate a half-turn halfway through the cooking time.
— Trim the frogs' legs and sprinkle with the breadcrumbs; cover and cook at 70% for 3 to 4 minutes. Remove the cover, give the plate a half-turn and continue to cook at 50% for 4 minutes, or until cooked.
— Trim the lobster claws, cover, and cook at 70% for 5 minutes. Give the plate a half-turn and cook for 5 to 7 minutes longer, or until completely cooked.
— Arrange equal amounts of each seafood around a serving of rice on 4 plates.
— Cover the plates and reheat, individually, at 70% for 3 to 4 minutes.
— Reheat the garlic butter and serve separately, giving your guests the option of using it or not.

Crème Royale

Ingredients
375 mL (12 oz) milk
3 eggs
45 mL (3 tablespoons)
sugar
2 mL (1/2 teaspoon) vanilla
4 macaroons
15 mL (1 tablespoon)
apricot jam
2 oranges
2 slices pineapple
250 mL (1 cup) 35%
cream, whipped

Method
— Heat the milk at 100% for 4 minutes, stirring after 2 minutes.
— Combine the eggs, sugar and vanilla; whip vigorously while slowly pouring in the hot milk.
— Crumble 3 macaroons and add to the milk and egg mixture.
— Pour into a greased round mold, place on a rack, and cook at 70% for 8 minutes, stirring three times during the cooking. Let cool.
— Pass the apricot jam through a sieve to extract the syrup; heat the syrup at 100% for 40 seconds.
— Turn the custard out of the mold and pour the syrup over it.
— Cut the oranges and pineapple into thin strips, crumble the remaining macaroon, and sprinkle these ingredients over the cream.
— Garnish with whipped cream before serving.

MICROTIPS

Wines To Serve with Seafood

Although there are no fixed rules about what wine to serve with seafood, it has generally been our tradition to serve white wines with fish and shellfish. In this spirit we shall offer some suggestions as to which white wines are particularly appropriate with seafood.

The muscadet family of dry white wines from the Loire go especially well with shrimps and mussels. The flavor of escargots is perfectly matched by an Aligoté, a Mâcon or a Sylvaner.

A white Beaune or a Riesling suit lobster dishes while any Chablis is ideal with oysters and frogs' legs. The flavor of seafood dishes served in sauce, such as Coquilles Saint-Jacques, is greatly enhanced by a white Graves or a Meursault.

Seafood Terminology

Beard: To trim any fins, filaments, tentacles, etc. from seafood.

Byssus: The bundle of filaments situated at the hinge of the two shells of a mussel that permits the mussel to attach itself to rocks. The byssus should be removed before cooking.

Caviar: Salted, preserved sturgeon eggs.

Cephalopods: A family of mollusks without shells, including squid, cuttlefish and octopus, characterized by a group of muscular arms about the front of the head.

Coral: Rose colored eggs of the female lobster. The coral is edible; its special flavor is much appreciated.

Court bouillon: A liquid flavored with white wine, vegetables, and seasoning in which fish and crustaceans are cooked. The court bouillon can be stored and used for several recipes, or it can be used as a base for a soup or white sauce.

Devein: To remove the intestinal track (the black vein) from the shrimp.

Fish Stock:	Court bouillon, to which fish trimmings (heads and bones) are added. It can also be prepared with shellfish and other seafood.
Flake:	To lightly crush seafood or fish meat with a fork.
Pen:	A rudimentary shell inside the squid that emerges as the head and tentacles are separated from the body.
Plastron:	The ventral part of the shell of the crab.
Salt water:	Sea water or salted fresh water, used to cook fish. Salt water should be used only for freshly caught fish.
Sepia:	A black liquid, also called ink, secreted by octopus, squid and cuttlefish for protection.
Shell:	To remove the shrimp from its carapace.
Skin:	To remove the skin.
Trimmings:	All parts of any fish or crustacean that are removed and used as a base for fish stock.
Trunk:	The body of the lobster.

Culinary Terms

Have you ever been faced with a menu and found yourself unable to understand the terms used to describe certain dishes? Of the many culinary terms that exist, the majority are French in origin. To help you understand the vocabulary, here is a short list of culinary terms and their meanings:

à l'américaine: with onions, shallots, tomato and tarragon. Widely used with lobster.

à l'armoricaine: with garlic, tomato and oil.

à la bordelaise: with bone marrow, shallots and wine.

à l'espagnole: with oil, tomato, pimento, onion and garlic.

à la florentine: with spinach and, in most cases, cream.

à la grecque: with olive oil and lemon; frequently served with a sauce made of white wine, celery, dill and coriander seed.

à la hongroise: with onions, paprika and white wine, and sometimes with tomato paste.

à la Newburg: with cream, sherry and fish stock. Widely used for lobster.

duxelles: a mixture of finely chopped mushrooms, shallots and onions, sautéed with dry white wine. Frequently used as a filling or to accompany fish and shellfish.

mirepoix: a mixture of cubed carrots, onion, celery and spices. Used to enhance the flavor of seafood or meat.

papillote: a method of cooking fish, wrapped in oiled or buttered paper.

Conversion Chart

Conversion Chart for the Main Measures Used in Cooking

Volume
1 teaspoon............ 5 mL
1 tablespoon......... 15 mL

1 quart (4 cups)....... 1 litre
1 pint (2 cups)...... 500 mL
1/2 cup............ 125 mL
1/4 cup............ 50 mL

Weight
2.2 lb......... 1 kg (1000 g)
1.1 lb............... 500 g
0.5 lb............... 225 g
0.25 lb............. 115 g

1 oz................ 30 g

Metric Equivalents for Cooking Temperatures

49°C..............	120°F	120°C..............	250°F
54°C..............	130°F	135°C..............	275°F
60°C..............	140°F	150°C..............	300°F
66°C..............	150°F	160°C..............	325°F
71°C..............	160°F	180°C..............	350°F
77°C..............	170°F	190°C..............	375°F
82°C..............	180°F	200°C..............	400°F
93°C..............	200°F	220°C..............	425°F
107°C..............	225°F	230°C..............	450°F

Readers will note that, in the recipes, we give 250 mL as the equivalent for 1 cup and 450 g as the equivalent for 1 lb and that fractions of these measurements are even less mathematically accurate. The reason for this is that mathematically accurate conversions are just not practical in cooking. Your kitchen scales are simply not accurate enough to weigh 454 g—the true equivalent of 1 lb—and it would be a waste of time to try. The conversions given in this series, therefore, necessarily represent approximate equivalents, but they will still give excellent results in the kitchen. No problems should be encountered if you adhere to either metric or imperial measurements throughout a recipe.

Index